Access Your Free Bonus Content

Welcome to Voice Teacher Influencer!

PLEASE NOTE:

I have created online video lessons and downloads to assist you with studying this material.

There will be points in the book where I will prompt you to find a supplemental video lesson or downloadable resource in your book member's area.

Please go to **johnhenny.com/bookbonus** to register and access your free bonus content.

Voice Teacher
INFLUENCER

VOICE TEACHER SUCCESS SERIES - BOOK 2

Grow Your Studio, Increase Your Authority,
and Make More Money

JOHN HENNY

Also available in the Voice Teacher Success series:

Teaching Contemporary Singing

CONTENTS

INTRODUCTION

So here you are, congratulations! You have taken that all-important first step by acknowledging you are a voice teacher who wants to receive more from your teaching life—whether that's more time with your friends and family, more peace of mind, more talented students, more authority and influence, and more impact and global reach.

Perhaps you also want less as well. Less stress, less worrying over your bank account, less fear of losing students to competitors, less wondering, "Why can't I have a product or book?", less fear of what others think, and less frustration watching other teachers do better than you.

My goal with this book is to help you reach these goals of more success and less stress. It is my sincere wish that you experience the heights of what teaching can bring you.

Now, if you'll permit me, I want to brag a little bit—and those who know me know that this does not come naturally to me! In fact, for most of my life, I took great pride in people telling me how humble I was. (Wait, can you be proud of being humble?).

But I now realize that if I don't tell people my story, who will? So here goes a bit of horn-tooting:

Would you like to work with some of your personal heroes? I have.

Would you like to be featured in important publications? I have.

Would you like to meet and learn from the leaders in this industry? Yep, I have.

Would you like to be invited to speak at prestigious events? Uh huh.

Would you like to see your name as an Amazon bestselling author? Yeah, it's pretty awesome.

Would you like to earn thousands per month in passive, while-you-sleep income? Indeed, I do.

Would you like to charge more (much more) than many of your competitors? Right again.

Would you like your ideas and methods to be influential far beyond your local studio and area? Yes, this can happen to you as well.

A good friend of mine, Jamie Vendera, has created his own vocal empire from a small town in rural Ohio. He has appeared on international television, worked with rock superstars, written bestselling vocal books, and launched a successful online course—all from his home studio in a town very few people have even heard of!

The explosion of the internet has changed everything, and voice teaching is no exception. It has opened up the opportunity to succeed from anywhere in the world. However, voice teaching (and voice teachers) tends to be resistant to change.

Why is this?

Some of it has to do with this being a tradition-rich craft that goes back hundreds of years.

We talk in reverence of Bel Canto and the Golden Age of Singing. This tradition is wonderfully rich and full of wisdom—but sometimes this tradition can be slow to adapt and change.

We also have fast-moving developments in voice science, as well as the need to teach singers how to successfully (and healthily) work in the current commercial styles of singing.

Add to this mix the total disruption that the internet has brought to this industry (as it has to so many others), and you have people's heads spinning!

I want you to unspin your head and embrace what is happening. It's not always easy or pretty, but the truth is always the best place to start. This book will take you on a journey and show you how to embrace these changes and grow your business in the new Millennium.

The internet has literally rewired our economy and society. Your ability to reach and influence people from all over the globe has dramatically shifted. But remember, it has changed for the consumer, as well.

Think about how you make a purchase now. Even the most mundane things such as laundry detergent have hundreds of reviews, from professionals to consumers alike, all available with a few keyboard strokes.

How many times do you search through Amazon reviews when making a decision? I know I do. What's amazing is there is no rational reason to believe that most of these people have the authority and knowledge to review this product—and yet, we trust them. Why? Because we are social creatures, and the opinions of others matter whether we want to acknowledge it or not.

Your potential students are the same. They have the means and ability to research a great many voice teachers at the touch of their phone. Your online presence and reputation are now of more impact and importance than ever before.

You are no longer competing with just those in your area. The option to give lessons over free services such as Skype and Zoom has completely revolutionized the landscape.

Wait, you don't like Skype lessons? Don't think they work as well? Doesn't matter! Consumers make the decisions here, and a certain percentage of them prefer long-distance lessons for a variety of reasons.

This means you have competition from teachers around the world who have embraced this technology. This also means if you think Skype lessons don't work, then you need to educate the potential student as to why it's best to meet in person.

Another huge change is the constant influx of new voice teachers into the industry, especially in more densely populated areas.

Every year, schools graduate many more voice majors than there are singing jobs. There is also the fact that voice teachers can often charge more than teachers of other instruments (much to the frustration of guitar teachers everywhere).

This has led a large number of underemployed singers to hang up their shingle and promote themselves as voice teachers.

But there is another catch to this glut of teachers. Consumers are also more suspicious in the digital age—more suspicious of our leaders, news sources, and yes, you, the voice teacher. You cannot simply open your doors and expect people to trust you with their time, money, and voices. You need to establish authority.

Wait, you say, I have a degree! I belong to a prestigious vocal organization!

Unfortunately, that doesn't work as well as it used to.

For reasons I will explore later in this book, it now takes more to get the average person to choose you over another teacher. Some people argue that universities have less influence in the current digital age, and many of the movers and shakers of our society and business do not have degrees. In fact, many of the most successful contemporary voice teachers I know do not have a vocal degree.

I want you to embrace the current marketplace realities because resisting them changes nothing—except the chances of you finding your version of success.

Employing these strategies and tactics will advance your authority and expertise quickly, so I have one thing to say about this now:

Make sure you are good at what you do and keep growing and getting better!

The one mistake you can make right now is using the strategies I show you to grow an authority that's simply not there. You have to be good at what you do!

Now, this doesn't mean you have to wait until you get the approval of your peers. In fact, this is a huge mistake I see teachers make that I will address further in these pages.

For now, get good at the craft and art of teaching. Do an honest appraisal of your current skillset and get the education and training you need to bolster your weak spots.

Now let's see if this book is right for you.

*

So, who is this book for? This book is for you if:

1. You want to teach better, more gifted students.

Serious voice students are going to be choosier in selecting their teacher. They will do more research, and they will want to know you have the skills they need. In this book, I will show you how to present your skill set so these serious students will want to choose you as their teacher.

2. You want to be more mobile.

One way to become a very successful teacher is to open a studio and stay there ... for a long time. I know teachers who have moved away from their studio but now commute because of how well established they are.

But what if you want or need to move further away? Now you are forced to reestablish yourself without the benefit of having spent years building up a reputation, connections, and community. You land in a new town where no one knows you—and where competitors want to keep it that way. I will show you how to quickly pass them by and become the go-to authority in your area.

3. You want to charge more.

This is a touchy subject amongst voice teachers. There is a lot of debate about the right way to charge for your services, and I always say charge as much as your market will bear—and a little bit more! You should be the most expensive teacher in your area. It is hard to be your best self when you are struggling financially. Let's face it: you should be fairly rewarded for the VALUE you bring to your clients.

4. You want passive income.

Trading time for money is a treadmill that is hard to get off, and it will never bring you true wealth, no matter how much you charge. I'm not suggesting teaching voice is the path to riches (although for some it is); rather, I'm saying that there is a better way to structure your time without giving up income. You can even increase it while giving yourself more free time!

Time for your family, time for your health, time for inner work (meditation, prayer), time to give to your community, time to study and become a better teacher, time to perform. The bottom line is that you need time away from the studio to accomplish these goals—time away while you are still earning money. I will show you how I did this.

5. You want a greater reach and impact.

You can reach billions of people online, with billions more being added in the coming years. My podcast is heard in places such as Iraq, Cuba, and Uganda—places I never imagined reaching and influencing as a voice teacher!

You have the ability to help singers all over the world. Through the internet I have been able to connect with some of my heroes. Recently, I even got the opportunity to work with Penn Jillette of Penn and Teller. I have been a huge fan of Penn for many years and his approach to critical thinking and humor has been a huge influence for me.

I started working with Penn online, which is an amazing story itself! I recently spent an evening with Penn, just the two of us (at his invitation). We hung out, discussed music, performing, and life. It was a bucket-list moment for sure!

I don't write this to name-drop (although name-dropping is almost required of Los Angeles voice teachers), but rather to show you what's possible when your influence reaches beyond your own area.

Now, for whom this book is *not* intended.

First off, let me start by saying that there is no problem in not wanting to embrace the concepts I lay forth in this book. I believe knowing who you are and what you truly want is an incredibly vital life skill, and the approach I lay out in this book is not for everyone.

I would also like to add this disclaimer: I truly respect my fellow voice teachers. If you teach voice, then you are in the service of helping others achieve their dreams, and that is something pretty special. What follows in these next paragraphs is not meant to offend, but rather to give you, the reader, clarity on whether or not you should continue reading this book. Your time is precious, and I don't want to waste any more of it than I already possibly have.

This book is not for you if you are looking for teaching techniques or pedagogy. I'm going to show you how to grow your business, not how to teach. If you would like to expand your teaching skills, then I would like to humbly recommend my first book in the Voice Teacher Success series, the bestselling *Teaching Contemporary Singing*. This book is not for you if you are perfectly happy teaching the student base you currently have, at your current rate.

This book is not for you if you are uncomfortable with pushing forward and taking risks, often with accompanying criticism. This IS NOT for everyone. I know fantastic voice teachers who work part-time from their home, with no desire to grow, because it fits their chosen lifestyle. I know great teachers who keep their fees lower than they could charge because they feel it's the right thing to do. They like being affordable for their students.

Staying in your safe space is not what this book is about. I will be pushing you to go beyond your comfort zones and to explore additional revenue streams. You will be asked to work harder for periods of time in order to experience more free time and profit down the road.

This book is not for you if you believe voice teachers should wait their turn, climb the appropriate ladders, and earn their place in the teaching hierarchy. This is where I may turn some of you off completely, but I advocate you to take your turn *now*. You need no one's approval (and often won't get it) to grow your business and, ultimately, your brand.

Again, I want you to constantly improve and train—but you can get your business growing *right now*, with the skill set you currently have. In fact, with the strategies I will show you, you can grow your studio and reputation much faster than previously possible.

It's up to you and no one else.

Marketing legend Dan Kennedy has pointed out that the best people in any industry are often the poorest. It's not about being the best, but being *perceived* as the best. These are the people who are the most successful.

Does this upset you? It used to upset me, greatly.

In fact, there was a time when this book would not have been for me. To be brutally honest, what I am writing and advocating now would have totally frustrated and pissed off the younger me! I thought the teaching world should be fair and reward skill over self-promotion and perception. But just as in life, there's little fair about it. Once I accepted this, I was able to see true growth in my business.

I will tell you my story in the next chapter, as I think it may resonate with some of you. And, as you will find out, your story will become very important to your brand and ultimately to your success. If you connect with me and my story, you are more likely to listen to what I have to say, and ultimately, you will be more likely to purchase services and products from me.

I don't recommend trying all the tactics and strategies in this book to start. Read the book all the way through, and then go back and focus on the areas of influence that interest you. Take small steps, build on your successes, and learn from your inevitable stumbles.

So what is a Voice Teacher Influencer? Synonyms for "influence" include "sway," "impact," and "authority." Influence will give you the ability to sway potential students to your studio and products, to impact vocal education with your unique ideas and approach, and to have the authority to reach singers all over the globe.

By becoming a voice teacher influencer, you will be in greater control of your studio and career, with the ability to explore paths of which you might now only dream.

I believe each of us has something special to bring to the world of voice. There is a gift within you that can help singers everywhere. Your growing influence will be the key to getting your gifts out there and making a difference. In doing so, you will be justly rewarded. Your future audience is waiting for you now.

Chapter One
MY STORY

I stumbled upon voice teaching in a rather disjointed way. It was not a straight path by any means—much more like a squiggly line. And, believe it or not, it all started with a drum set.

It was Christmas morning, and in the weeks leading up to the big day, all I had asked my parents for was an air hockey game (Hurricane Hockey!!!). It was one of the hot toys that year, and my parents had a hard time finding one. So, in a selfless act of desperation, they bought me a used drum set instead!

Now, I had wanted a drum set for as long as I could remember. As a young child, I would watch the bands at the old Disneyland Tomorrowland Stage (the one that rises up from underground). Oh man! I loved that! I would position myself behind the stage so I could watch the drummer.

I would stare at their hands in amazement. The blur of the drumsticks, the flying feet on the pedals, the cymbals crashing and vibrating in the air… This was for me!

But I never thought my parents would go for such a loud, crazy instrument. So I would take my piano lessons (which I hated) and carry on with typical tween activities like skateboarding and collecting baseball cards.

That Christmas changed my life. I remember coming down the stairs and seeing this glorious drum set. In that instant, all of my desire for Hurricane Hockey was gone.

I was now a DRUMMER!

And drum I did. Every day after school, I sat there for hours and hours as I played along to my favorite albums.

I ended up studying with legendary drum teacher Freddie Gruber (who also taught Neil Peart of Rush), and I went on to play professionally starting in my teens.

But then came another fateful day.

I was in my early 20s, and a roommate came home and announced he had started voice lessons with a teacher who mentored under Stevie Wonder's voice teacher.

Boom! Stevie? I was in.

I had always wanted to sing but never thought I had any talent for it—a fact that had been drilled into me by my Scottish-born Glaswegian father who would proclaim my attempts at singing as "Bloody TERRIBLE!"

I know this may come off to the reader as cruel, but as the child of parents born and raised in Scotland, this is just how we would express affection—by yelling at and insulting each other!

But regardless of the hard time my dad always gave me, I made the decision that day to schedule my own voice lesson.

There were no websites in those days, so I got the teacher's number and gave him a call. His name was Eric Futterer, and he was a perfect fit for me. Smart, empathetic, encouraging, yet able to criticize and correct at the right moments.

I flourished under his instruction, and I moved from behind the drums to lead vocalist in just a few years. Yep, I was now making my living singing!

I ended up getting a record deal that ended with the band going down in flames. I'll spare you the gruesome details, but this left me at a crossroads—do I pick up the pieces and chase my rockstar dreams again? Or might there be something else?

As fate would have it, I began studying with Eric's mentor, the legendary Seth Riggs.

At the time, Seth was teaching just about every superstar in Hollywood, including Michael Jackson, Prince, and Madonna—oh yeah, and me!

As I diligently worked with Seth, he saw potential in me and suggested that I start teaching. Even better, he informed me that he had just begun a training program for teachers.

So I jumped in with both feet and started to climb the teaching ladder.

I studied like crazy and soon became a top-level teacher. At that point, I began training other teachers around the world to be certified Speech Level Singing instructors, which was an absolutely wonderful experience!

Within this system, I had a good reputation and an automatic flow of enthusiastic teacher trainees and students. I traveled the world presenting masterclasses and sharing these contemporary singing techniques with singers and teachers of all levels I was busy, successful, and happy.

Then, for various reasons, I decided to move my studio closer to Hollywood. It was time to leave the organization behind and strike out on my own.

JOHN HENNY

This is where the story changed for me.

I was now completely alone in the hyper-competitive world of Los Angeles voice teachers, and I saw a new reality apart from the confines of my former experience. Here, teachers weren't ranked by their actual skill set, but by how many celebrities they had taught. I was stunned and angered as I watched teachers—who were quite mediocre and with nowhere near my training or experience—blow right past me on the success ladder, racking up celebrities and raising their rates beyond what I could have ever imagined charging.

I felt angry and frustrated. I would rail against this culture of mediocrity to anyone who would listen. I felt I deserved their success because I had worked so much harder at my craft. I knew I could teach better than many of them—*much* better, in certain cases. In fact, I had attempted to train a few of them, and I knew how limited their understanding and skill sets were. Yet they kept rising right past me.

Now, this is not to say I didn't experience my own level of success. My studio continued to grow by word of mouth (though not as fast as I felt I deserved), and I eventually worked with a fair amount of celebrities, as well as brilliant session singers and voice actors. But I was still frustrated by these teachers who out-promoted and out-hustled me.

I then made a fateful decision, one that would change my life more than I could have ever imagined.

My studio had grown to the point where I felt that my reputation and client list was enough to open my own music academy. So with eyes closed and wallet open, I created a 2,000 square foot, state-of-the-art facility, complete with a recording studio and fully equipped stage room, to entice singers and musicians to learn at the best school around.

And what happened? My wallet stayed open and money began pouring out. This dream quickly became a financial sinkhole. Turns out, my ego had completely miscalculated what it would take to fill the place with students.

4

Wait a minute! I had read the important voice books and attended, and even spoken at, the right conferences. I had written articles for major publications like *Backstage Magazine*, and lectured at the Paul McCartney Institute of the Arts and USC. Didn't people *know* they should attend my school?

No, they didn't. And worse, they didn't care.

Not only was the school draining my bank accounts, it was also impacting the time I could spend at my own private studio. So I was being financially impacted on both ends.

Then I had an idea—because, you know, my ideas had been so great up to this point!

I decided to create an online training school for voice teachers. This is what I knew, and I had had great success in this area, so Voice Teacher Boot Camp was born.

But again, I faced the question: how do I get people to sign up? Luckily, I had enough reputation amongst voice teachers that I was able to get initial subscribers with little effort. This became a source of income to offset the losses at my school, but I knew this couldn't continue for long. I either had to make the brick-and-mortar academy a success, or close the doors and accept my losses (which would have been substantial).

So finally, and reluctantly, I began to look at marketing. Yep, self-promotion and a bit of hustle. The very thing I had disdained in those "lesser" voice teachers was now something I was being forced to accept. It felt dirty and against everything I thought should be right about the world—achieving success on your skill level and merits, not on hype and elevator pitches.

However, the world is rarely "right," and it was in this moment I needed to embrace the realities of this industry. I needed to become a marketer. As I would come to find out, marketing is not the most important thing—it's the *only* thing.

I quickly launched myself into the world of Facebook Ads, sales funnels, content marketing, webinars, and more products. And very quickly, something happened.

By employing what I was learning, my music academy stopped losing money, and then it started making money. In fact, I was able to triple my revenues within 18 months. A stunning result.

Now I was hooked. I realized why these other voice teachers were more successful than me, because on some level they understood marketing and self-promotion. Looking back, they weren't even that good or sophisticated at it, but they were doing something while I was doing nothing. I sat with my entitlement while they went out and built their businesses.

In this book, I will show you a way beyond what those voice teachers did, and it will most likely be far beyond what your competitors know or are implementing (a big difference).

If you study and, most importantly, implement what I show you, you will blow by your competitors, including those who have been teaching in your area much longer than you. You can expect them to react as I did, with disdain and criticism, but I will encourage you to react as those teachers did with me—by not caring and pressing on.

I don't want you to be the bitter version of me, but rather the happier, more successful one!

Chapter Two

THE VOICE TEACHER TRAP

We voice teachers all share a desire to be good—good singers, good teachers, and good colleagues.

Singers must quickly learn to please an audience. This also turns into a need for acceptance, a need that a bass player usually doesn't experience. If the bass player doesn't connect with an audience, few in the audience will care, as he or she is not the main focus. If the singer cannot connect, you likely won't have another gig.

Teaching voice is also different from other instruments in that it takes an especially empathetic and emotionally supportive approach. Other instruments can be played well even if the player is a bit stressed or feeling a bit negative. Many a piano player has suffered under a stern teacher and been perfectly fine, but the same style of teaching is often far from effective when it comes to singing. The nature of the human instrument, and the fine control we need over muscles not completely under our awareness, is a delicate balance that is thrown off by stress. We need to be more positive and emotionally connected with our students than most teachers.

This creates an environment where voice teachers struggle when it comes to delivering criticism and judgment. You would think performing on stage would toughen us up, but the opposite is often true. We are wired to connect and please.

Marketing can put this entire mindset at risk—you will need to put yourself out there and withstand the slings and arrows that will indeed come. I don't say this to scare you, but rather to prepare you, because the rewards are so much greater than the small and ultimately insignificant criticisms of trolls or a few tightly wound peers.

There are some ideas and myths I want you to put aside right now. Even if you believe some of them, they will not serve you going forward. They will only keep you stuck in place, and your reach will be stifled.

Myth #1: Serious Voice Teachers Do Not Market

The argument is if you are good, your studio will be full no matter if you market or not. I have heard teachers brag about never doing a lick of marketing, and some of them are arguably successful.

But this is not entirely true. Marketing is simply making people aware of you and your services, and these successful teachers do this consistently by going to events, networking, putting out content, being at community events and performances, or reaching out to local schools— this is all marketing in some form. What they really mean is they don't do *paid* marketing. I would argue your time is incredibly valuable, and this type of marketing is taking your time.

I encourage you to be active in your area and network as much as possible, but that being said, there are paid avenues that can make things happen more quickly for you and on a larger scale.

It's also important to note that some of these teachers have been in the same location for many years, which acts as a kind of passive marketing all on its own. This is great for them, but most of us need to find a way to build our reputations without being tied down.

Myth #2: Fear of Criticism

This is the one area that if I could snap my fingers and magically fix it for you, I would.

Worrying about other's opinions is death to your growth as a business person. These fears will stop you every step of the way, from product concept, to launch, to pricing—everything you need to be doing fearlessly.

I remember the bitter version of me, watching these "lesser" teachers have great success and somehow thinking my disapproval of them should mean something. It didn't. They rightfully and correctly did not care about my approval. Could they be better teachers? Yes, but were their skills so poor they did not deserve the students they were getting? No.

But let's say they were so poor that the students were being done a disservice—that I, or another teacher, could save them from impending vocal damage. Was I doing these singers any good by sitting on the sidelines and complaining?

No. I needed to out-market and out-hustle these teachers in order to make singers more aware of me. I needed my reputation and authority to be delivered to them, rather than sitting back and hoping somehow they discovered me.

Which leads to the next trap:

Myth #3: Word of Mouth Should Be Enough

Personal recommendations are the best source of new students, and I welcome and encourage them. However, people are busy, and even your most enthusiastic students aren't always going to do enough of it for you.

People are overwhelmed and focused on themselves, so they are not thinking of you and your business. They also might not recommend you for selfish reasons, such as keeping you away from one of their competitors. It's indeed frustrating to have a student brag they won't tell others about you because you are their "secret weapon."

Waiting for recommendations is also putting the growth of your business in other's hands. You need to be proactive if you want to explode your business and influence. While you should encourage referrals, and perhaps even create a reward system for students to refer you, it cannot be the driving engine for real, sustained growth.

Myth #4: Being Good Should Be Enough

It should be—it really should. And it will be when I am given the supreme powers to create my own perfect universe, but for now, in this reality we live in, it sadly is not.

As we mentioned in the introduction, marketing legend Dan Kennedy says that it's not about being the best, but being *perceived* as the best. These are the people who are the most successful in any market.

We love to romanticize the undiscovered genius. We love to hear stories that brilliant artists like Van Gogh whose paintings go for millions of dollars were broke, or how Mozart was buried in a pauper's grave. But you know what? It sucked for Mozart.

Being good or even the best is not enough—you need to be PERCEIVED as being the best. Argh! How unfair is that? But it is completely true.

But why can't you put a new spin on this unfortunate reality? Why can't you be incredibly good AND do the marketing to be perceived as the best? It can (and does) happen, but there is still the stigma of marketing and "hyping" your skills, and some will accuse you of not being as good as you say you are simply because you are well-marketed.

Tell them you would like a slightly better gravesite than Mozart.

Myth #5: Fear of Pricing

Voice teachers are, at their core, artists. Artists and capitalism have been waging a long war, and they don't sit well together.

There is the temptation to look at what others are charging—the highest and the lowest—and to price yourself somewhere between them, often towards the lower end, especially if we are new to an area.

There is also a feeling of guilt in charging top-dollar to students, which often equates to a fear of being greedy. But I want you to think of your pricing in a new way.

Don't think of your price as a dollars-for-minutes transaction where you sell your time, but rather as the value you bring to the singer. If you are able within the course of a few lessons to give the singer a vocal breakthrough, what is that worth? A lot!

Also, if you price your services too low, you risk devaluing the experience in the mind of the singer.

Take McDonald's French fries, for example. Most can agree that when they are prepared just right, and you get them fresh and hot, they are sublime little torpedoes of junk food bliss. But it's McDonald's. They are cheap, and though they are enjoyable, it is not a special occasion for you or your mouth.

Now imagine sitting in a beautiful and very expensive steakhouse. If you were served these very same fries alongside your perfectly cooked, marbled rib-eye, they would be elevated because of your perception. You would pay more attention to the flavor and likely savor them more. The same is true for students and lessons.

If simple french fries can be elevated by perception, so much more the gold that is your teaching.

As you create a sense of being the best, pricing plays an essential role. If you are in the middle of the pack, you might make the bargain hunters happy, but the perception of your skill level and authority can be compromised.

You may miss out on working with higher-level singers because of the perception created by a lower rate.

When you pay more for something, it becomes more special. Have you ever taught someone for free? Were they your most dedicated student? Often the answer is no.

Charging more also gives you the freedom to offer scholarships to deserving students. You are less effective when you are broke and struggling—less effective for your family and loved ones and less effective as a teacher. I will argue your financial success can make you a more confident and effective teacher, and will make your students more engaged and focused.

Myth #6: Doing The $10 An Hour Jobs

We all do it, getting stuck doing the mundane tasks of running our studios. Scheduling, returning emails, chasing down payments—all of these can be done effectively by people for much less than our hourly rate.

You need to value your time as much as, or more than, those who pay you for it. When you are doing low-wage tasks, you are robbing yourself of your true value and putting your business growth to the wayside.

I know it's much easier in the moment to do a task yourself instead of training others, but in order to truly grow, you need to think more like a CEO. Remember, executives pay others to do the smaller things while they create and strategize.

Your favorite singer is not moving the gear from gig to gig—this would be a waste of his or her time, and their performances would suffer from exhaustion. The singer needs to focus on their performance. They need to deliver their best to you—which is the most valuable job of all.

Let others do the $10 an hour jobs while you do the $200 to $1,000-an-hour jobs. I will cover this in a later chapter on outsourcing.

If I can do a one-hour webinar and sell $2,000 worth of product, should I be worried about returning phone calls to students? Is this where my time is best spent?

As I write this book, I know this is a higher-level job that I cannot outsource to others. A book will boost my perceived value and credibility like few other endeavors, so I am happily up before my family awakens, pounding away at the keyboard.

These are the types of jobs you should be focused on - teaching (although you can outsource that to teachers under you, I will tackle that later in this book) and business growth. The jobs that only you can do.

Myth #7: Never Enough Time

Trading your time for dollars means you will likely never have enough of either. While I can show you ways to grow your profits, I cannot give you more than 24 hours in a day—but we *can* find ways to better utilize that time.

The best way I have found is the magic of passive income, or creating products that make you money while you are spending time with family, traveling, or sleeping.

I will confess, it's a wonderful feeling to find you have made as much overnight as you would in a full day's teaching!

Product creation does take an initial investment in terms of learning how to create and market, but it is well worth it. We both know there is a product or course in you that needs to be unleashed for the world to enjoy!

I will argue you are doing yourself and the singing world a disservice by not creating your product or book, and we will discuss this at length later on in the book.

Chapter Three

YOUR MINDSET

The right mindset is critical in order to push yourself out of your comfort zones and on to greater success.

There is another book to be written on just this topic alone (it might even be my next book, in fact!), but for now I will go over the essentials you need to drive your business forward.

Reinvest in Your Business (AKA ABUNDANCE)

The concept of abundance is extremely important. Abundance is the opposite of scarcity, which is where many voice teachers operate. It's easy to get stuck in a scarcity mindset—whether it's students leaving your studio for one reason or another, competitors setting up shop down the street, or not enough hours to do what you need to do - it all adds up to frustration and fear.

Abundance, on the other hand, is realizing there are more than enough people who want to learn to sing, and that there is more than enough money for you to earn what you need. It is all there for you to get, without shame or guilt. Your success takes not a crumb of food from someone else's mouth—in fact, your success allows you to affect greater change in the world.

A very important part of abundance is investing back into the business. When acquiring new customers or students, the person willing to spend the most to acquire the student will win almost every time—especially when expanding beyond their immediate area.

I think of the money I spend on marketing not as an expense, but as an investment that brings back a return. It's what brings students to my classes and enables me to do what I love to do.

Marketing Is Everything

This is a constant theme in this book, and I want this buzzing around in your head like an annoying song. Marketing is the engine that will drive your business and your income.

At its very core, marketing is simply showing people what you do and how it can benefit them.

Rest assured, I will show you how to market in an ethical way that creates value for the prospective client and raises the perception of your authority and expertise. The goal is to have a marketing system that your audience enjoys and benefits from while bringing you the clients you can best help and serve.

You Deserve The Life You Want

I have worked with voice teachers who had massive waiting lists, which to me is a huge sign that they were not charging enough. When I suggested they raise their rates, they told me they couldn't because another local teacher (who had been teaching longer) didn't charge that much. These teachers kept their rates artificially low out of a sense of guilt and waiting their turn.

There should be no guilt in creating the life you want. If you can achieve it, then by my definition, you deserve it.

Teaching one-on-one lessons can be extremely rewarding, but again, it's very hard to achieve significant financial return by trading your time for dollars. By thinking beyond the studio and beyond the lessons, not only will you exponentially increase your income, you can vastly increase your opportunities to travel, lecture, influence people, and work with amazing talent—it's all there for you, but you need to believe you deserve it!

It's Your Turn

Seth Godin wrote a book called *What to do When it's Your Turn*, which I highly recommend you read. I mean, finish this one first, then go get his!

Perhaps most importantly, the subtitle of the book is: *And it's Always Your Turn*. Godin drives home the point again and again that each of us is special, and we all bring something different to any area.

You and I may both teach voice, perhaps even the same styles, but the experiences and supplementary skills we bring are ours alone.

I have performed thousands of gigs, not just as a singer but also as a drummer. I have done a fair amount of recording and songwriting as well. These experiences afford me certain viewpoints when working with singers, such as knowing tips and tricks to get through all kinds of performing conditions, how to sing and play at the same time, how to write songs for your voice, and breaking down rhythm and phrasing from my years as a drummer.

Think over your musical life up to this point. What have been your highs and lows? What do you feel are your special gifts, experiences, or viewpoints? Do you have a unique way of explaining or teaching?

I am no voice scientist, and there are a number of teachers who know more about voice science than I do. But I have a way of teaching the basic, applicable science to other teachers that makes these difficult concepts easier to understand. It has become a reason other teachers seek me out.

You too have something unique and special to offer... I'm sure of it.

Godin stresses that once we acknowledge that we have something unique and special to offer, we need to stand up and take our turn. We need to take a risk and show the world our special gifts, knowledge, and approach. I know there is something you can show me as a voice teacher that I do not know, at least not in the way you do. I also know your knowledge can help inform my students and broaden my teaching. I also know I will never learn what you have to teach me if you don't stand up and make yourself known!

It's your turn.

Avoiding Ladders

This subject is a dicey one, and there's a chance it may upset some people. Ladders are necessary at times, but I want you to avoid them as much as possible—or at least understand why you are climbing them and when you need to get off.

I have had ladders placed in front of me at various times in my life, and I myself have placed ladders in front of others.

What is a ladder? It is a system that requires you to follow the predetermined steps and levels that others have created, thereby forcing you to wait your turn.

Universities are ladders, delaying your career while you go through their system of approval.

Corporations have their own systems of ladders, holding back responsibilities and higher salaries until you are promoted up the rungs.

My first real teacher training was a ladder, a system of levels from beginning teacher to mastery. I was required to take two years of education and pass testing to ascend to each higher level. Later on, I was the one judging other teachers as they went through the ladders.

Did this help me become a better teacher? Arguably. Did this hinder me at some point? Undoubtedly!

Why? Because ladders can make you stall. They can make you feel like you are not ready, even when you are. I turned down opportunities I should have taken out of deference to my place on the ladder.

Ladders exist in more than just formal organizations. There are many professional and social ladders that you simply do not have to climb.

Yes, anyone can be a voice teacher simply by proclaiming themselves one, and this can be a point of frustration for more experienced teachers. Does this lead to some poor teaching? Of course. Does this mean you need to wait until others have decided you have climbed enough rungs of the ladder? Not at all.

You can decide to raise your perceived value and expertise right here and now. All it takes is bold action.

Again, a warning: If you truly do not have the teaching skills to back up your claims, I urge you to get them. Perhaps even climbing some ladders for a short period of time will be beneficial, as long as you do it with full awareness and avoid hindering the growth of your business and reputation.

Stepping up and offering your unique skills, without waiting for the approval of others, that's what I am talking about. Show me what you are truly good at and go get better at the things you are not.

I'll be waiting for you to show me those new skills!

Time Is Your Most Precious Gift

All the voice teachers I know are strapped for time. They spend time preparing lessons, teaching those lessons, scheduling students, returning phone calls and emails, attending performances—all of which take time. And with the exception of teaching the actual lessons, most of it is unpaid.

This leaves precious little time for their own education, never mind vacations and travel. Every moment spent not teaching is money lost—and this doesn't make time off as much fun!

Finding ways to recoup your time is worth your time—literally! Investing in systems that will allow others to do the $10-an-hour jobs will free you up to focus on what really matters. Creating passive income through products will allow you to travel while still having an income. Not having to grind as many hours in the studio will allow you to enjoy teaching more.

When you get your time back, you get your life back.

False Evidence Appearing Real

I used to watch Celebrity Rehab with Dr. Drew, and the craziest season was the one with Gary Busey. Gary has a "unique" view of life and reality, to say the least. I remember at one point the subject of fear came up, to which Busey replied: "FEAR is False Evidence Appearing Real." Wow! Did I just learn an amazing life lesson from Gary Busey?

Turns out, he is absolutely right—unless it is the necessary fear of impending physical harm, most fear is our old lizard brain reacting to needs and dangers that are not real or in the moment.

It used to be, many thousands of years ago, the tribe or group was critical to our survival. If we were cast out from the group, we would suffer alone to die some horrible death. Our brains still have this fear ready to spring up and tell us we will die without the approval of others. This is no longer true, of course, but the fear is still alive and well. This is the same part of your brain that will push us to seek sugar, salt, and fat in excessive amounts because these foods were so hard to come by until only very recently. The lizard brain has not yet adapted to modern life.

There is no longer a physical threat to your well-being if others don't approve of you, yet the fear remains—but as my guru Gary Busey points out, it is totally false.

Which brings me to the next limiting mindset…

Dealing With Your Critics

Criticism is so very painful, and I should know, as I have gotten my fair share. When I was just teaching in my own studio, I received little criticism (that I was aware of). I taught students who were happy and told me so. There was little reason for others to know much about me.

That changed when I started putting out content on the good old world wide web—and let me tell you, the critics were waiting!

I have been publicly called a "hack," been fat-shamed (that was especially mind-blowing), had peers critique me for selling courses and for training voice teachers outside of their ladders, and all manner of other painful attacks.

But underneath the criticisms, I sought to look for truths. Was I overweight? Yes, I needed to take better control of my health. Did I oversell occasionally? Yep, I had to admit that as well.

One instance in particular was after a webinar. I use webinars to teach on a subject and then offer an opportunity to work more closely with me, whether through purchasing a course, lesson, etc.

I had another voice teacher (whom I respect) attend this webinar. I gave what I thought to be good, solid information. I also shared some personal stories to cement the information and to help people identify with my struggles (remember, your story is important to others), after which I made the offer to purchase my course.

When I finished the webinar, I had made great sales and received positive responses. I was feeling very good about how it went until I saw this teacher comment that he was frustrated. Apparently, he felt the webinar was the equivalent of an infomercial.

This stung a bit, as I truly respect this teacher. I had just received a number of "thank yous" from other teachers about the webinar, yet this criticism erased all of that in my mind.

However, I knew I had to sift through and see if there was anything I could have done differently.

I realized his reaction was caused by being sold to at the end of the webinar—without a fair warning that this would be happening. Upon reflection, I decided to change my approach. To create a better, more open experience for those watching my webinars, I now let people know there will be an offer after I teach for an hour and they are welcome to leave at that time.

Now this goes against a lot of marketing advice for webinar structure, but voice teachers tend to be more educated and aware (we are just plain smarter than mere mortals!). I had to adjust to my audience, which is a key aspect of marketing.

I am still able to conduct financially successful webinars, but now with the peace of mind knowing my audience will not be caught unaware when I make an offer to work more closely with me. This greater level of transparency has worked out very well.

Now that we hopefully have our mindset a bit more in order, it's time to start establishing and growing your authority.

Chapter Four
ESTABLISHING AUTHORITY

Authority will be one of your most valuable business assets. Authority will enable you to more easily attract desirable clients and to sell your courses and products.

What is "authority" and how do you acquire it? For our purposes, authority is being regarded as the go-to expert in a certain area or specialty. It's not about being the world's greatest voice teacher, although some do try and lay claim to that ridiculous mantle. It's also not about feeding the voice teacher ego.

Ultimately, it's about helping others, usually in a smaller niche of the voice teaching universe. And the *helping* part is absolutely essential. Although it may seem counterintuitive at first, helping people and being of service is the key to gaining authority.

Establishing Influence and Authority

Establishing authority is a critical piece of the marketing puzzle that most people get wrong. When we think authority, we naturally think of our credentials. It is my degrees and affiliations that bestow authority upon me, and therefore they are what establish me as the expert in the consumer's mind.

Here's a cold hard truth: most potential students have no way to truly evaluate your expertise because they aren't good enough at singing to know what true expertise is. The very fact that you have a sign outside your door that says "Voice Teacher" will cause most people to assume your expertise. Credentials help, but only so much.

Imagine you have been falsely accused of a terrible crime and need an attorney to save you and your reputation. How do you choose the right one? By looking at the initials after his or her name? By analyzing to which attorney groups this lawyer belongs? Probably not. You would already assume they know how to practice law on a competent level, yet this is likely not enough to help you make your decision.

What do you need to know in order to trust this attorney with your future? As you scan different attorney websites, what is your mind screaming out for?

HOW CAN YOU HELP ME??? Me, me, me. You do not care about education or awards—you care about specific results with cases like yours. Results with real people like you.

Now, I know you might want to argue that attorneys have to pass the bar and there is a minimum requirement of regulated skill and testing, unlike voice teachers. But the public, by and large, does not know this nor do they care. The assumption is if you are in business as a voice teacher, you have the requisite level of skill.

Now back to you and your impending prison sentence: In looking at the websites of different attorneys, you see page after page extolling these attorneys' experience. How they worked at this prestigious law firm or graduated from that elite program. But it's all about them and their achievements—it's not about you. And you need things to very much be about you right now. Your freedom depends on it.

25

You then Google your specific charges and an article appears on the best way to plead your specific type of case. Are you going to read it? Of course.

The article is easy to read and includes some great, actionable information that gives you peace of mind. You see this article was written by an attorney who has handled a number of cases involving your exact situation. As you go through the website, you see case studies and testimonials from people who got their charges dismissed or greatly reduced because of this particular attorney.

At this moment, is where this attorney went to school the primary thing on your mind? Is this going to be what drives your decision? Probably not.

The difference is, this attorney made it all about you. Your needs, fears, and desire for freedom. The article helped provide a solution to your specific issue, coupled with real-world proof of success, which created a sense of authority and expertise in your mind so strong they could have gone to a diploma-mill school and you would still likely pick them.

THIS is the type of authority I want you to create. It takes a bit of time and some work, but it is something other teachers in your area won't do—or if they do it, they won't do it well.

Creating authority in a chosen area will allow you to attract the type of student you most want to work with. It will allow you to charge more for your services (you expect to pay more for a cardiologist than a general practitioner, after all).

This authority can also carry over to other income sources such as teaching webcam lessons, speaking engagements, workshops, as well as passive income streams such as online courses.

In order to best focus your efforts, we are going to want to identify your particular niche and the person you are most able (and willing) to help.

What are you most passionate about when it comes to teaching singing?

Who do you connect with most?

What problems do you have a gift for solving?

This does not mean you cannot work in other areas—I'm sure you are great at a few key areas of the voice—but starting with just one or two will allow you to become an authority in that area. You'll be a specialist rather than a general practitioner.

Some key areas could be:

- Musical theatre audition prep
- College auditions
- Finding a singer's unique style/artist development
- Vocal rehab
- Recording a great vocal/vocal production
- Developing young voices
- Working with older voices

The list goes on.

Even though I do a lot of work with singers, one of the areas I am known for is teacher training. This is an area I have a passion for, and I have spent a good deal of time creating my own authority in the space.

Once you have a chosen area, you need to know who you are going to be talking to.

This is where something called the "customer avatar" comes in. You are going to create a fictitious, composite persona and you are going to focus on THAT person. You are going to solve that singer's specific problems. If your avatar is a singer-songwriter, his concerns are different than if your avatar is a teenage girl who wants to audition for her dream college. Even if you train them in practically the same way, you would approach each of them with a different language and focus.

The more you can speak directly to a specific person, the more that person, or those very much like this person, will flock to you and your product.

This book is for voice teachers who want to learn how to market themselves and expand their reach and influence. There are voice teachers who find this somewhat distasteful—very good, respected voice teachers who do not like marketing.

I started this book by talking about who this book is for—my avatar or ideal client. The fact you are still reading means you are likely a very close fit to my avatar, and I am speaking directly to you. You are my people, the ones I want to help, which means there is a higher likelihood of you purchasing something from me in the future than from another person selling marketing courses.

The concept we are going to use is content or information marketing. I am secretly and not-so-secretly marketing to you throughout this book, but I am doing it by giving you some of my absolute best information. I am not holding things back in order to drive you to buy because by giving you some of the best of what I know and use in my business, I increase the chances of you wanting to work with me and my team.

And if by reading this book you decide I am not someone you want to work with, that is a positive for both of us. Take what works for you, apply it, and leave the rest behind. The perfect person for you to work with is out there, it just may not happen to be me.

Let's take the next step and create your customer avatar.

Chapter Five
THE CUSTOMER AVATAR

I want you to think about your perfect client. They can be based on someone you have worked with in the past, or it can be a combination of previous or current clients. This is the person we are going to target, and we are going to make an effort to get to know them better—MUCH better than we already do. We will accomplish this by creating a customer avatar.

So, what is an avatar, exactly? An avatar is a breakdown and a composite of your ideal customer—their likes, dislikes, problems, fears, what they like to read, where they want to hang out, and so on. The reason for this is the more we can define the exact person you are talking to, the better you can create relevant content and marketing to drive this type of person to your studio or program.

Think of a client who perks up your day. Think of the sessions where time just flies by. Think of the student who you would gladly teach for free. Let's get more of those!

I want you to create an avatar that embodies the qualities of this student, as well as their problems and objections.

Here's an avatar for which I wrote this book. Now, you likely aren't this exact person, but you might find bits of yourself in the avatar.

What IS important is that the avatar gives me focus. It helps me decide exactly who I am talking to and what they most need to learn from me.

Here's my avatar:

> *Julie*
>
> *38 years old*
>
> *Married, two kids (ages 7 and 9), both in school which gives her more free time*
>
> *Has a degree in music performance, has done regional theatre. Feels this should bring her the type of students she wants to work with but it's not working as well as it should*
>
> *Loves to help kids prep for auditions*
>
> *Likes to work with younger children*
>
> *Once had a student go to Hollywood Week on American Idol. Would like more of these very talented students.*
>
> ***Goals:*** *Wants to grow her teaching studio, attract better students, raise her rates.*
>
> ***Problems:*** *Overwhelmed by the technology choices*
>
> *Fear of critics*
>
> *Has tried blogging but not sure how to do it well*
>
> *Tried FB ads but did not help*

Marketing makes her uncomfortable, feels tacky

Afraid of raising her rates when she still has openings

Dreams of writing a book and having a course on auditioning but no idea of how to start

She is willing to invest in growing her studio and influence but is afraid of wasting money

By having Julie as my avatar, I can stay on message and not wander into information that's not relevant to her. I can speak directly to her concerns and help solve her specific problems.

I want to encourage Julie to reach for her goals, so it's important that I am able to effectively answer any objections she may have. I want to address her fears and reservations of putting herself out there, and I want to help her find the proper mindset to go forward. I also want to give Julie a small vision of her future self—a future where she has more free time, professional satisfaction, and additional income.

My customer avatar guides my voice in writing this book. It informs the subjects and chapters as well as the overall tone.

My avatar will also guide any social media posts or advertising I do to promote this book. I will speak directly to Julie—or at least as she exists in my mind. Any further offers for courses or one-on-one coaching will be focused and created directly for her.

My avatar creates a cohesive voice and flow to my efforts and keeps me from trying to be all things for all voice teachers.

You can have more than one avatar, but for now I would stick to just one or two.

And remember, just because you are speaking to a single avatar, this will not exclude other potential clients who are not exactly like your avatar. Rather, it will give you the best chance to reach your ideal student.

I have created a customer avatar worksheet you can download at johnhenny.com/bookbonus

Fill out this worksheet and keep it where you can refer to it often. The more you can connect with this person, the faster you will grow your influence and audience.

Chapter Six
THE CUSTOMER JOURNEY

Now that you have an idea of your audience, you need to understand their journey. That is to say, you need to understand their decision-making process when it comes to signing on with you as a student or client.

Gone are the days when potential clients would open the Yellow Pages and pick the teacher with the biggest ad. The sheer amount of information and the ability to research choices has changed the way people make big decisions, like investing in voice education.

You need to think of establishing a long-term relationship with your potential client.

We've all met people who come on too strong, those pushy salespeople-types who want to be close friends a bit too fast. This immediately sends off alarm bells because human relationships need to follow an organic path. Think of being on a date: if the person touches your hair before they have touched your arm, it's likely to come off as too forward.

Establishing a customer relationship follows similar rules (but without the creepy hair touching thing!). First we need to introduce ourselves, then create a level of trust and authority before asking for a sale.

We also need to make sure the path we set out for the potential student makes sense. If any part of the journey is confusing, or makes them have to think too hard, they are likely going to bounce.

This means that all of your marketing, website, information, and courses need to follow a logical progression and branding so the client knows what to do next.

Take the frustration of "click bait." You see an interesting headline and click, thinking you are going to read an article, only to find the "article" is just a bunch of ads and pop-ups. Completely annoying.

Yet many voice teachers have created their own version of this annoyance—they will send prospects to pages on their site that are confusing, or to pages that look like they are from another website. Their contact information is hard to find, or it's just a list of their credentials with nothing to show how they can help the student.

I've seen music teachers post on Facebook that they now offer group lessons—but the link goes to their homepage with no mention of group classes or how to take the next steps to work with them.

Teachers create long, meandering blog posts that talk about ten different things, with densely packed paragraphs that are hard to read on a phone.

They offer signups to a newsletter, but don't tell anyone what to expect in the newsletter—or even worse, they never actually send out a newsletter, ever!

All of this combines to create a poor customer journey. I don't want this for you or your business. We need a system that shows how good you are and what you can do for singers in a clear, easy-to-follow path. Keep the customer journey and its logical progression in mind as you lay out the next steps to building your influence.

For most teachers, this will start with their website.

Chapter Seven
YOUR WEBSITE

With today's easy-to-use templates, building your own site is much easier than ever before. However, I recommend working with a web designer so you can focus on the more important tasks of creating content and building authority. That being said, I would suggest you learn enough to make small changes on your own. Nothing is more frustrating than having to wait weeks for a webmaster to change two words on your site—and then being sent a bill for it!

But I don't want to talk to you about how to build your site, but rather about the overall experience of the user. This way you can explain to your designer exactly what you want your site to do.

Perhaps most importantly, you want the flow of the site to be easy to read, especially on a mobile phone, since this has now become the way people primarily use the internet. For this reason, you should spend a lot of effort getting your homepage just right.

The Homepage

Your homepage is now more crucial than ever. In fact, many effective websites are simply one-long homepage, due to the scrolling nature of the phone. Menus are more cumbersome on a phone, so you want as much information as possible on your first page.

Your homepage should include a picture of you, somewhere near the top as people like to see faces. You can include your credentials in a quick, easy-to-read manner so they can verify that you are qualified. As I stated before, most people will already assume you are qualified, but being able to quickly glance and reinforce this is a good idea.

You then want to have testimonials and social proof. Show that you get results from real people. You also want to talk about how you can help singers and highlight the specific problems you can solve.

The homepage is not the place to go in-depth on specific issues. You will save this for your blog page.

You also want your contact information front and center. I recommend having it on the homepage, near the bottom.

Another effective touch is to put a short video of yourself welcoming the visitor, and a second video talking about you and your approach to singing and teaching. You want to instantly create a bond of trust between you and the visitor and the more they can see and hear from you, the better.

You should also be aware of another type of page.

The Landing Page

Landing pages serve a very specific function on your site and in your marketing. They may or may not show up in your menu and may not be reachable by any way besides a direct link. Why would you want such a page?

I see a lot of voice teachers make a HUGE mistake by running an ad (about a specific offering, a group class, or a special on private lessons, etc.), but when potential clients click on the ad, they are taken to their homepage, which has no specific information about the offer.

Most visitors to your site will leave before taking the time and trouble to figure out where they should be. The landing page solves this for you.

The landing page has only a single objective: to get the visitor to take action. It is designed to cut out distractions or any other decisions beyond the one you want them to make.

For this reason, landing pages usually do not have a menu at the top of the page or links to other pages. The landing page exists on its own to serve its single purpose.

For example, if you are driving visitors to your site in order to take advantage of a special offer or to sign up for a free eBook, the entire page should be focused on getting the decision you want. The text and any clickable button are all in sync to drive your marketing message or to deliver your content.

If your desire is to get someone to sign up for a free consultation lesson, then that's all the page should focus on. Everything else is a distraction and a decision-killer.

Branding and Design

Another mistake I often see voice teachers make is giving no thought to cohesive design in their brand. Your website (as well as all your online presence) should have a unified look and feel.

I have seen websites where the colors and fonts change from page to page, almost like each page is an entirely different website. This can create a confusing user experience, and we NEVER want our visitors to be confused.

Your website will be a hub of content and information from which your authority will grow, and you will want it to reflect the same amount of professionalism and attention to detail you bring to your teaching. This is where an experienced web designer is invaluable.

Be sure to discuss your customer avatar with your designer to help with the overall look and color scheme.

I suggest getting a logo created for your brand (yes, you are now a brand). This can be easily outsourced to Fiverr. Use this logo on your social media pages and videos as well.

Everything you create, from your website to your content, should be communicating who you are as an educator. Just as you would never have your studio be a confusing, disheveled space, you want the same levels of professionalism and thought to everything you do online.

Next, we will look at how to create effective blog posts to bring traffic to your site and students through your doors.

Chapter Eight

BLOGGING

The very mention of blogging makes most voice teachers groan. They envision the constant grind of writing articles that sit ignored on their site, getting no comments.

And I must admit that most voice teachers are pretty bad at writing blogs—the information is often great, but they usually don't get read.

Why is this? Because the way people consume content online is different from this book or a research paper. When you consider that most people will read your blog on their phone while dealing with distractions, you can see the need for a different style of writing and delivery.

The most common mistakes I see on voice teacher blogs are:

1. Poor choice of headline: Your headline is essential for helping the reader choose if this is something they want to read, as well as for search engines to display in their results. This is not the time to get overly cute or clever. Your headline should specifically address what the article is about.

Poor headline: The Air That I Breathe

Better: The Top Three Ways to Improve Your Breathing

2. Written in an overly technical, non-conversational style: Remember, potential clients may be reading your article on their phone while standing in line at the grocery store. If it looks like a slog to get through, they will instantly jump to Facebook or some other diversion.

We are in a battle with online ADD. As I write this on my laptop, I have to shut off all alerts on my computer because I can't have anything else fighting for my focus. Your reader will likely have not taken these steps, which means that you are in competition with everyone who mentioned them in a Facebook comment.

Keep your writing simple and to the point. Imagine that you are talking to someone sitting in front of you. Don't worry about the grammar police or writing for your peers (big mistake). Talk directly to your avatar.

3. Too dense: This is an extension of the previous point. Easy-to-read blogs have no more than a few sentences per paragraph, and often just one.

Why? Because of the nature of reading while scrolling on a phone. Larger paragraphs are harder to read and can cause the reader to bounce away to something less taxing.

This paragraph will be a bit daunting to read online because it is too dense, with no space between the words. As I go on and on about various ideas, there is no space to give the reader a chance to pause and reflect; the information just keeps coming. It is also harder to "chunk" or take in the knowledge in bite-sized pieces, and the densely packed words and sentences don't work well for someone who is scrolling on their phone. Also, they are getting constant interruptions in the form of email, social media alerts, their environment, etc. It will be harder for the reader to remember where they were in this long paragraph. Also, as the mind wanders, they can easily lose focus in this uninterrupted paragraph. The reader will look at a paragraph like this and most likely bounce from your page, missing all of the vital information and help you are trying to give them, eliminating you from their mind as a teacher they might want to work with. As long as this paragraph is, I've seen voice teachers go on much longer, thinking the sheer number of words will make their posts more interesting and valuable, but as I am hoping you see here, it often has the opposite effect.

In contrast, you want to use small paragraphs. Often just one sentence can work perfectly fine.

The use of **bold words** can help bring out the **important points** you want to **establish** in the **reader's mind**.

The use of bullet points can bring:

- Clarity
- Focus
- Help reestablish takeaway information

Hopefully you can see the difference in readability. Always think of your reader and make the information useful and easy to understand and read.

4. *Making it about you*: I know I am drilling this point over and over, but it's critical. If you take one thing away from this book, it should be the realization that ALL of your focus should be on the potential client or avatar. Be their problem-solver. Even if they don't become a client, you will likely be top-of-mind when someone asks them for a recommendation.

One of the most egregious examples that I have seen was a blog post supposedly to help students get over the disappointment of auditioning and not getting the part—a good blog topic, for sure. But this particular teacher made the post all about *her* experience, which is still not a horrible premise as long as there is something for the reader there. Personal stories can be a powerful way of connecting with the reader.

In this blog post, however, the voice teacher talks about not getting a role and contacting those running the audition to ask why (not something I would recommend, but that's another story) only to find out she wasn't chosen because … wait for it … she was TOO PRETTY! That was her whole point. Sometimes beautiful people like her are just too good looking to get the job.

Now, is this a post that is going to resonate and solve problems for the average singer? I think not.

While this is an extreme example, I want you to constantly put yourself in your reader's shoes and read anything you write from their perspective. Make sure you are giving them value and showing them you are the ultimate solution for their particular problem. You don't have to be salesy—just have good content.

5. *Not solving a specific problem:* Don't try and take on too much with a single blog post. If you have a subject that can be broken down, then by all means break it down! If you want to talk about vocal health and nodules as part of the discussion, consider having a blog post just about vocal nodules.

If a singer is worried about possibly having nodules, they will be far more likely to click on and read an article specifically about that issue rather than one where nodules are buried in a bigger subject.

Side note: Write articles to attract the types of singers you want to work with. If you have experience in dealing with vocal issues and enjoy working to help get singers back to health, then this type of article is perfect. I know a very gifted voice teacher who has helped rehab singers, but he ultimately finds this work less interesting as it requires a slow, steady pace. His passion is helping elite singers take their voices to the highest levels, so an article on nodules would not bring him the clientele he wants to ultimately work with.

6. *Trying to write too much:* If you are a prolific writer, great! Keep typing away. But the point I want to make is that you do not need to be releasing

blog posts every day, every week, or even every month. If you can create a handful of compelling pieces that are easy to read and truly helpful, you can get a lot of mileage out of them.

In order to drive your studio forward, you are going to need time and energy, and I don't want you getting bogged down in blog writing. We want to use every resource to the best of its ability, and getting burned out by writing 50 blog posts is not going to get us to our goals.

Every post should ultimately have a specific goal for you and speak to a specific client you want to attract. We then want to drive readers to this post and create as much attention as possible from it. Ultimately, too many posts are going to dilute your attention and resources. Make each post count.

7. *Not pixeled*: I didn't say "pickled," but "pixeled." This is a special piece of code, usually from Facebook or Google, that will tell Facebook someone has visited your site—even which page they have looked at. This will be critical down the road in building audiences to run ads to. Yep, I said run ads, because paid advertising is going to be essential if you want to explode your studio beyond where it is.

I will go deeper into the Facebook pixel later in this book, but for now, suffice to say it will be incredibly important.

Note: I will be focusing mainly on Facebook in later parts of the book because it truly is the 800-pound gorilla in the social media space. You may (and should) ultimately want to branch out and build audiences on other platforms, but for now, I recommend starting with Facebook.

Another note: When referencing an article, book, or other sources of original knowledge, it is always good practice to put a link to the source material. No one likes their work used without credit. Also, always be respectful of use rights and never ever plagiarize another's work. It can get you a bad reputation very quickly.

These blog posts will serve as a beacon for your avatar, a solution to their most pressing problems—namely, you.

The work you put in here will pay you back many times over with a growing audience of singers who are enthusiastic to learn from you, whether through private lessons or paid courses.

Once we have valuable, helpful content on our site, it's time to start building our list and making sales.

Chapter Nine

LEAD MAGNETS AND TRIP WIRES

Lead magnets and trip wires may sound like top-secret military gear, but they are actually great ways to build your email list and customer base. These devices will create a friction-free path for your audience to become fans and, ultimately, paying customers. It's all about providing an experience where each step leads logically to the next.

The Lead Magnet

A lead magnet is the common internet marketing name for a premium freebie. This takes the shape of a valuable piece of information that you will give in exchange for a person's email address.

Quick note: changing privacy laws have made it more and more important that you have the user's permission to receive emails from you. NEVER add someone to your email list without permission or buy email lists from third party sources. Always give people an easy way to opt-out of your list at any time.

Common popular lead magnets are:

- Special reports
- Short eBooks
- Checklists

The lead magnet should solve one specific problem: don't bog the reader down with too much information. Save it for another lead magnet.

There are a number of ways to host and distribute the lead magnet automatically. LeadPages is a popular service that will create your landing page as well as sync with your email service provider and deliver the lead magnet to your audience.

After getting an email from the lead magnet, you want to start delivering quality content to your list, building rapport and trust (see the chapter on email lists for more information).

The Trip Wire

This is a rather aggressive-sounding name but it's a very important step in turning a subscriber into a customer.

The trip wire is a very low-cost offer (usually around $10) that creates a low barrier of entry to taking the first critical step of becoming a paying customer.

I can still remember the first purchase I made on Amazon back in the late '90s. Amazon only sold books back then, and I was looking at an edition of Arthur Rackham's illustrations of Wagner's Ring Cycle operas. I hesitated for quite a while, not sure if I wanted to give my credit card to this new, somewhat unfamiliar website.

But the price of the book was right, so I took the plunge and clicked "purchase."

Today, I am an Amazon Prime member, with five Echoes and two Firestick TVs. I have monthly subscriptions of common household items such as toothpaste and, as I look around my office with its furniture, printers, and TVs—all of it came from Amazon.

That small step of buying a $12 book now has me spending many thousands of dollars a year with Amazon.

Your trip wire is that critical first purchase—a leap of faith and trust for your customer. Each subsequent purchase will now be easier for them.

Considering the customer journey, the trip wire should be a logical next step after the lead magnet. If the lead magnet was The Top 10 Audition Mistakes, the trip wire could be a short video series or eBook on how to prepare for your next audition.

This then sets the customer up to want to buy your larger $297 course on complete audition techniques.

You will bring the customer along through logical steps of free, small price, larger price—building your authority all the way (because your content will be amazing!).

The technical part of doing all this can be intimidating at first, but with the advent of all-in-one services like Kajabi or Teachable, it's not that difficult.

Of those who buy your core $297 course, there will be a percentage that wants even more from you—and this is where private coaching, masterclasses, and even subscription membership sites come in.

The key to this whole process is making each step an easy, logical advancement from the previous one. You want to make sure the progression makes sense for the buyer.

I wouldn't have a lead magnet dealing with auditioning and then try to sell a trip wire on R&B riffs and runs. You will get greater sales if you make the next step focused on musical theatre.

Of course, you can have multiple lead magnets, each leading to a different trip wire and then a more expensive course, but I recommend you start with one audience and one path for now.

Just like learning to sing and ultimately to perform, you need to get out there and see how your offerings work in the real world (much like stepping on a stage). As you create and build your audience, you will get a better idea of what they want and will ultimately purchase from you.

Chapter Ten
VIDEO

Video is currently the most powerful way to connect with others, and there is now more video being watched on Facebook than on YouTube. Video is immediate and personal, helping to create an instant bond with the viewer.

It is also the medium that tends to strike fear into the heart of the person being filmed. I have worked with confident, successful, outgoing voice teachers who go into tongue-tied shock as soon as the camera is turned on!

While voice teachers are often accustomed to performing, the idea of just being themselves on video can be intimidating. If this is a bit nerve-wracking for you, the best bet might be to just start off with blog content and then work your way up to video as you get more comfortable with your offerings.

I launched my first product during the stressful time when my academy was losing buckets of money every month—and the stress showed. I was horribly overweight and certainly didn't look how I would like, but I made the videos anyway, and nobody cared. I knew not to make it about me but about the information I was giving to people. The lesson?

Whatever worries you have about appearing on video is of no concern to anyone else.

Video is also a great addition to your info marketing arsenal because it can be used in so many ways. Live broadcasts, webinars, demonstrations in a blog article, courses—video is king when it comes to delivering content.

We are all social beings who like to see others. People will often watch videos of a podcast rather than just listening to the podcast itself. People with headsets talking into a mic? Yes, not a lot of action, but we connect better when seeing a face, hence the name FACE-book.

A quick note about YouTube: While the site has the largest potential audience for your videos, this is not where I suggest starting your efforts unless you are already comfortable and somewhat skilled with video. YouTube is quite competitive and viewers can be a bit harsh, particularly in the comments section, so be ready for a lot of trolling.

You don't need much fancy equipment to get going, except for one area—sound. Even then it doesn't need to be overly expensive, but I highly recommend getting a lapel mic for your camera or phone. Viewers will forgive less-than-perfect lighting and camera work, but bad sound will annoy the viewer quickly.

I even use a lapel mic when doing Facebook Live broadcasts. It may be me holding my phone with less-than-steady video picture, but the sound is clear and easy to listen to.

I have created a list of my favorite video tools for you at johnhenny.com/bookbonus

How to Approach the Camera

Since you teach singing, my guess is you have performing experience, so this part shouldn't be too hard for you. Here are some key guidelines for interacting with the camera.

First, make sure the camera is at eye level or a bit above. It's not usually a great look to have the camera looking up your nostrils!

Second, treat the camera like it is a person you are talking to.

I once worked with a top voice-over artist who did loads of national commercials (if you live in the US, you've heard her voice). I asked for her best advice for aspiring VO artists, and she responded with a question:

"When recording a commercial, how many people are you talking to?"

I took a guess and said, "Millions?"

"No, just one. Talk to just one person."

The camera needs to be that one person. Know where the lens is and focus your eyes and attention on it. Make the lens someone you are teaching, convincing, joking with. You are not afraid of discussing voice with a student or a friend—so don't be afraid of the camera.

Simply talk to this one person. Don't judge what you are saying, and, unless you are amazingly skilled with this, don't prescript and read your content.

Reading will almost always come off stiff and stilted. If I have a number of points I want to cover, I will create PowerPoint slides and use them to stay on track as I lecture on and discuss each topic. If I want to include the slides in my video, I can use a program such as Screenflow to record my camera as well as my computer screen for a very effective presentation.

Embrace Your Uglies

It's human nature to start judging ourselves when we first start doing video. Our weight, our voice, our mistakes and pauses—all of it can suddenly seem like a huge deal! My best advice is you simply have to let it go.

Drop all pretense of perfection and embrace your uglies. Those aspects of yourself you don't particularly like can and will endear you to your audience as long as you allow them to see the full, flawed, authentic you.

I have been all sorts of a mess on camera. My hair started to thin so I shaved it all off, suddenly completely bald. I've gone from being on camera overweight at 370 lbs to now being a bit strangely thin.

A 6'7" skinny bald man who occasionally makes a fool of himself on camera? You bet! I've embraced each version of myself and let it all out there. Do I always enjoy watching myself? Absolutely not, but I am not who I am trying to reach or help.

Make it about reaching those who can most benefit from your particular expertise, and let all the other nonsense go. Embrace your uglies, especially those parts of yourself you don't like.

Those who need your help don't care.

Remember the Path

When choosing a topic for a video, think about your avatar and focus on a specific problem you can solve within the confines of a single video.

Then, think of the path you are guiding them on. What action do you want them to take?

When you solve the problem, there should be a next logical step so you can help them solve even more problems.

If you have a course or a workshop you want to promote, make the topic of the video logically flow to the next step of wanting more information about your course.

It's very easy to get bogged down in each step of this path to establishing yourself as "an authority," so the key is to keep the 30,000 foot view and always be aware of the desired outcome you want for the potential student.

Start Now

I suggest you start creating video content as one of the first steps in growing your influence. With each video you record, you will gain confidence and a natural flow in front of the camera.

By leveraging the connecting power of video, you will be able to build an audience of people who like and trust you much more quickly and efficiently than with written content alone.

Chapter Eleven
EBOOKS

An eBook can be a great giveaway to people who visit your website, and it is relatively easy to do. Think of an eBook as an extended blog post, a deeper dive into a subject of interest.

I suggest getting a few blog posts up and running and seeing which ones generate the most interest. If you have a clear winner, this could be a great subject for a more in-depth eBook.

The eBook does not have to be extremely long—it can be as little as 2,000 to 4,000 words. As I write this book, I am averaging around 2,000 words during a 2-hour writing session, so you can easily write your eBook in a couple of days.

The eBook usually has one specific purpose: to build your email list. An email list is an important part of your overall marketing strategy, but people are less and less likely to part with their personal contact information these days. An email address has value both to you and the person visiting your site, so you should offer something of value in exchange for it.

The typical voice teacher website will have an email opt-in to subscribe to a newsletter. Except for very rare circumstances, the average person is not looking to sign up for another newsletter. Why? Because a newsletter is a vague promise of future information that may or may not be useful.

Also, how many people actually put out a newsletter on a regular basis? Very few.

The eBook is a better driver of opt-ins precisely because it solves a specific issue. Again, don't try and make your eBook too broad. Keep it focused on solving a specific problem for your ideal client—your avatar.

If you have a large number of blog posts, you can make an eBook out of a collection of posts. Again, I would find a unifying theme that brings the posts together that would be of specific interest to the student. Doing this can make the production of your eBook really simple since you already have the content.

There are programs that make formatting an eBook easier, as well as services that can help you get everything polished and ready to send out. Fiverr is a great option to find someone who can assemble your writing into an attractive, downloadable document. I will discuss this more in depth in a later chapter, but the more work you can outsource, the more important work you can get done.

By providing an eBook of value, you will get greater value in return— a growing list of potential clients and buyers.

Chapter Twelve

PODCASTING

Podcasting is one of my favorite ways of establishing authority with potential clients. It is fun and relatively easy to do, and it's a great way to find your audience and build them into an eager group of followers (and purchasers) of your services.

Podcasting has an advantage over platforms such as YouTube and Instagram because you do not compete for the audience's attention—other podcasts are not jumping into their feed to lure them away. When they listen, they are focused solely on *you*. You also OWN your podcast, unlike these other platforms.

I get thousands of downloads per month of my Intelligent Vocalist Podcast, and I have a consistent audience that considers me to be a vocal authority on some level.

The podcast has brought me a stream of people that sign up for my email list, purchase my courses, and study with me over Skype and Zoom. These people don't need to be sold to very hard because they have already spent multiple hours listening to me talk about the voice. They already trust me by the time they enter my sales funnel.

Another great benefit is that the podcast attracts the exact type of student I enjoy working with. I love students who are really serious about the voice (Who doesn't?). The material on my podcast has a thoughtful, science-based focus (hence the name, Intelligent Vocalist). This means my audience is pretty serious and ready to put in the work when they study with me. My favorite students now tend to come from my podcast audience.

One of the big mistakes new podcasters make is quitting before the podcast has a chance to really get going. Most podcasts fade after just six episodes, and I am here to tell you it's going to take a lot more than six episodes for your podcast to find its audience.

The most popular length of a podcast is equal to the average commute, about 20 to 30 minutes. Publishing weekly is also the best way to create a listening habit for your audience. If this is a bit daunting, go for at least every other week—but don't do less than once a month, or you really don't have a podcast.

There are exceptions to this. My friends Chris Johnson and Steve Giles have an incredibly popular podcast called the Naked Vocalist, and they can go months between releases. However, they supplement the podcast with in-depth blogs and a Facebook community, so they keep the audience engaged between episodes.

I started my podcast with little planning or thoughts of where it would go (I don't recommend this). I only did episodes when the mood struck me, and listener growth was slow. When I made the commitment to weekly episodes, however, downloads began to climb much more rapidly.

Another great benefit of podcasting is you can get each episode transcribed. (Rev.com is a great resource and provides fast, accurate transcriptions for just $1 per minute). These transcriptions not only become great show notes, which can help people find you when searching Google, but the content can be repurposed into blogs, social media posts, eBooks, infographics, and more.

What You Need

One of the great things about podcasting is that it is incredibly inexpensive. It costs as little as $5 a month to have your podcast hosted and sent out to all major channels such as iTunes, Stitcher, and Spotify.

You can get great audio results with a $100 microphone and a recording program like GarageBand. You can even use Audacity, which is free.

If you are truly technology-adverse, you can have your episodes inexpensively edited and prepared by finding an audio engineer on Fiverr.

I have created a list of recommended tools and programs in the online member's area for this book: johnhenny.com/bookbonus

How to Get Started

It's important to get clear on your style when you get started. Podcasts usually go one of two routes: you can be a solo act, or you can go interview style where you bring in different guests.

The interview platform is a popular way to go because it eliminates the need for you to consistently come up with new, unique content every week. It also allows you to build on the guest's audience.

Super tip: By inviting guests who already have a popular podcast (or other channel such as a YouTube following), you are going to bring in a certain percentage of their audience to listen to your podcast, and a number of them will likely become listeners of yours as well.

Having guests is a great way to build your audience with little expense or work on your part, and the guest will most certainly tell their audience about their appearance. They don't even need to be in the same room as you—Skype and Zoom are perfectly fine.

You will obviously need a title. Don't get too clever here—make it easy for someone to decide if this is a podcast that would interest them. It's better to name your show "The Singing Technique Podcast" as opposed to "Soaring Notes" or some other clever yet vague title.

Get your podcast cover art done at, you guessed it, Fiverr. Note that Apple has specific requirements for the artwork, so I would be sure to use someone who is familiar with creating podcast cover art.

Next, sign up for hosting. I use Libsyn because it is easy to use and simple to set up. Libsyn will house your audio and send it out to iTunes and other platforms where people can find you and subscribe.

You should have a page on your website to house all of your podcast episodes and show notes. A very effective technique for sending traffic to your site is to reference the show notes page and perhaps offer a free download that supplements that week's episode. This can be one of the lead magnets that we discussed earlier.

You should then record three episodes before you launch.

The first episode will be number 0 and will be a short explanation of what the listener should expect from your podcast. You will explain your intended style, what the format will be, some of the future topics you will cover, and so on. Think of it as a coming attractions reel of sorts.

You should then record your first two full episodes. Once you have all three episodes ready to go, upload them to Libsyn and hit publish.

You want at least three episodes so people can get a sense of who you are and your style.

Be Your Own Sponsor

I don't get enough downloads to attract sponsors, nor am I interested. I am my own sponsor. What do I mean? I put brief mentions for my own lead magnets, products, and services in each episode.

At some point during each podcast, I will tell listeners to go to my website for the show notes, links, or my offering of the moment. The offer can be a lead magnet, a small course, or perhaps an upcoming masterclass. This helps build my website traffic and email list, as well as sell my courses and services.

The return I get from podcasting is so effective that I now publish new episodes twice a week. As my business mentor James Schramko told me, the more you podcast, the more you sell. He was right!

Now to look at the ultimate authority builder: writing and publishing your book.

Chapter Thirteen
PUBLISHING YOUR BOOK

When building authority and influence, there is little better than having your own book. Being an author bestows instant credibility, more so than any degree or association. In fact, in our business, the only thing that rivals writing a book is celebrity clientele, which can be an elusive goal that is often dependent on location, connections, and other quirks of fate and luck. Writing a book, however, is completely within your control. (Plus, writing a book can help bring you higher-profile clients!).

Imagine being introduced at a conference as the author of "your title here." There is little else that needs to be said. You are now perceived as an expert by most everyone who meets you.

Your main objective in writing a book should not be to make instant riches. It's extremely hard to make money with a book unless you are John Grisham or J.K. Rowling. Instead, your book will be the best business card you ever create. Your book will lead people to seek you out as an authority in the niche for which you write it. Once again, I urge you to niche down and specialize. As your studio and reputation grow, you can reach out to a wider singing audience, but first it's important to establish yourself as an authority in a specific niche that you are both skilled in and passionate about.

Take this book, for example. It talks to a very specific group of people: voice teachers who wish to extend their reach and influence beyond the confines of their studio. By niching down I can talk to you in very specific terms, addressing your concerns, interests, and problems. In turn, I likely have your attention more than if you were reading a general small business or marketing book.

Writing A Book

Being an author not only attracts students and people who will purchase your products, but it can also put you on the radar of peers and influencers you might not otherwise get to meet.

A book is obviously a bigger undertaking, and while it might not be the first thing you should tackle, I want to get you thinking about it now. As you write and create content, you are going to become not only better and faster at your craft, but you are going to get a better idea of what your audience wants and how to deliver it to them.

While you are thinking about possible book subjects, start paying very close attention to questions you get asked again and again. For which problems do singers seek you out? What are your passions in the singing world? Where do student problems and your passions intersect?

While the prospect of writing a book may seem daunting, a non-fiction book on a specific topic can be as little as 10,000 to 20,000 words. In just an hour a day (and 1000 words per hour), you can have your first draft in just a couple of weeks.

The key is to outline your book carefully before you start typing, or you can quickly have a mess. You should pick a topic you know well so you don't need to constantly stop to research it (although checking up on yourself and doing some research is often a good idea).

Don't worry if you can't find a publisher. In fact, I suggest you skip the idea altogether.

The Self-publishing Revolution

There have been many disruptions in the internet age—Uber, Netflix, and AirBnB have displaced huge industries in ways we couldn't have imagined even just a decade ago.

But of all the disrupters, Amazon is king.

Retail has been absolutely devastated and our lives have been changed by the near-instant availability of a mind-boggling range of goods—most of which can be at our door in under 48 hours.

Another industry that Amazon has completely upended is the book industry, and it goes way beyond losing your local bookstore. (Ahh, this part does make me sad…).

The publishing industry has been shaken because Amazon is now a publisher in their own right, and they are open to all of us, not just established authors.

I have chosen Amazon to publish this book because a niche as small as voice teachers is not going to attract most publishing houses. By further segmenting potential readers to voice teachers who are brave enough to grow their visibility and influence, no publisher would likely be interested.

Enter Amazon. All I need to do is write my book, get it formatted with a professional-looking cover (hello outsourcing!), upload the documents, and BAM! I have both a Kindle and print version ready for immediate sale.

And the beauty of the print version is that Amazon handles everything, from taking the order to printing the book on demand, and shipping it out around the world.

My first book, *Teaching Contemporary Singing,* was a #1 bestseller in multiple categories and countries and I didn't have to print or ship a single one. Gone are the days of a garage filled with books you had to pre-purchase, or running to the post office with books you had to pack yourself.

And the best part is there are NO upfront costs. Amazon simply takes a percentage of each book sold.

Any excuse you have for not publishing a book is gone. It is now just up to you and your ability to get disciplined and start writing!

Note: The most important part of publishing a book is sitting down and writing it. I have a bonus chapter on Productivity available at johnhenny. com/bookbonus

Chapter Fourteen

REVENUE SOURCES

Almost all voice teachers would like to increase their income, but are often unsure about how to achieve this goal.

There are two basic ways of increasing your income: by attracting new buyers and by selling more to your current customer base, the latter of which is often overlooked in the quest for new students.

Some of these revenue sources will take a bit of time and work to implement, but there is one you can do right away.

Charging More

Let's start with the low-hanging fruit: your current rates. My guess is you want to charge more but are afraid of the potential fallout from clients. But worry not. I can tell you from consulting with a number of voice teachers that raising rates has rarely had negative consequences. In fact, the results are almost all positive, and not just from their own financial standpoint.

People expect to pay more for quality, and voice lessons are no exception. I previously lost high-profile clients because (I'm pretty sure) I did not charge as much as some of the other celebrity voice teachers.

The key is to create a sense of value so that potential clients feel justified in paying your higher rates. We tend to make most of our decisions on emotion and then justify these decisions with logic. By giving more perceived value, the student can logically justify the emotional decision of working with you (and paying a premium to do so).

Your higher price will also create a greater sense of value in and of itself, often attracting more serious and committed students. The higher price can be a boost to the student's focus and can help foster an environment of more rapid advancement.

At my music academy, we provide all of our books at no extra charge. We tell parents they will never have to worry about needing to run out and purchase a book, and when their child finishes one piano book, a brand new one will be waiting for them at their next lesson.

Does this cost me extra money? Of course. I have to spend about $10 to $15 every three to six months on each student. With hundreds of students, this is definitely a noticeable expense.

But what do I get in return? I use this perk or perceived value to charge nearly double what my competitors charge, and I get almost no complaints about my pricing. In fact, I have heard parents brag about how our academy is more special and of a higher level, justifying the extra pricing.

Of course, the books are not the only thing I do to create this sense of value, but they certainly are something my competitors do not do. This advantage provides me a very high return on my investment.

If you are uncomfortable raising your rates on your current students, go ahead and set new pricing for incoming students. Then let your current students know you have raised your rates but will hold their current rate for the next three months as a "thank you" for their loyalty. You might lose one or two current clients, perhaps, but you will more than make up for the lost revenue.

A quick word about potential students who push for a discount—seriously consider NOT WORKING WITH THEM! These students will more than likely be the most demanding and draining students on your schedule. In fact, raising your rates is a perfect opportunity to weed out those dreaded problem clients. You know who they are!

Upsells

I'm sure you have heard of the 80/20 rule, the idea that 80% of the benefit comes from just 20% of the work. This applies to your clients as well.

20% of your clientele can ultimately provide 80% of your income. This is because out of everyone you teach, you are going to get a percentage of superfans and superbuyers—those clients who simply cannot get enough of your teaching goodness and will purchase anything and everything you have to offer.

The problem is, most teachers don't have additional offerings beyond one-on-one lessons. Perhaps you have tried (or currently offer) group lessons, but these are usually aimed at beginners or less-committed students. Not a bad way to bring more potential students into your studio, but I am talking about offerings on a higher level.

Upsells can be a key area of growth for voice teachers—you just need to find the right offerings for your key clients.

What is an area of expertise you hold that is not fully utilized within your lessons?

Do you have skills in audition prep? Then you can offer a 6-week intensive on preparing for auditions (e.g., song choice, preparing resumes, and headshots) that is all capped off with a videotaped mock audition.

Have you written your own songs? A songwriting intensive is a great upsell. You can teach the basics of good songwriting in a group setting, leading to a showcase of your students' finished songs in front of a live audience.

If you have any level of experience with recording software, you can create a relatively inexpensive setup in your studio and start recording songs with your students. Start off with laying their voice over karaoke tracks, and then move up to helping them create their own original tracks and songs.

You can even build this up into an artist development program. I know teachers with choir experience who have created lunchtime choirs in the corporate workplace!

The list is as long as your supplemental skills.

Teachers Under You

This is often the first growth strategy that voice teachers attempt, and it is the one fraught with the most potential peril and danger. It is a danger to your reputation, business, and wallet.

I previously had a studio in partnership with another teacher, which brings its own set of issues I will touch on below. We would take students who couldn't afford us, or fit into our schedule, and give them to teachers who would split the lesson fee with us. For this, the teacher would not only get the client handed to them but also the use of our studio.

This worked out fine for a while, until the Monday I opened the studio to find a junior teacher's studio completely empty except for a "Dear John" letter stating she was leaving to start her own studio down the street. Even though we had an agreement that any students we had given them were to remain with our studio, I knew instantly we were getting screwed.

Indeed, this teacher had been contacting her (our) students over the previous weeks and letting them know of her impending move, so once I found out about it, it was too late. The students were gone.

What did we do wrong? Let me count the ways.

1. We allowed the teacher to have the student's contact information, giving her the ability to contact and convince them to follow her.
2. Upon conferring with a lawyer, we discovered our contractor agreement was not enforceable legally in the state of California.
3. When we pressed this teacher about the unethical behavior, she threatened to claim she should have been an employee rather than an independent contractor. She would not have prevailed in this, but we certainly did not want the hassle. Her threats worked.
4. We ultimately overpaid this teacher, providing the marketing, studio overhead, and our reputations (which brought the students in in the first place). Splitting 50/50 did not properly cover our costs of student acquisition and overhead, nor did it provide us a proper profit margin.

If you want to take on the task of getting teachers to work under you, I advise you to do much more due diligence than I did.

I now have a number of teachers working for me, but I have learned my lesson. Here are the things I learned the hard way:

1. All my teachers are employees, which allows me to control how they do their job. If you go the independent contractor route, be extremely careful how you handle your teachers. This is a legal gray area, and you can get into a world of hurt with the IRS, especially if you have an unhappy ex-employee. Make sure you discuss this with your accountant.
2. Don't do this if you can't bring yourself to fire people. You will have to let teachers go for one reason or another, and while it's never easy, it IS part of being a business owner and employer. The wrong teacher can quickly erode your business and reputation.

3. All student contact information is kept at my front desk and there is no contact between the teacher and student outside of the studio.
4. I make my studio an intricate part of the student experience, so there is little desire to leave and follow a teacher.
5. After doing the math, I realized I needed to keep my employee costs at around 35% of the lesson price or the profit margin is just not there. Remember, you are paying for systems, payroll taxes, marketing, equipment, insurance, utilities—don't be generous to the point of going broke.
6. Seriously consider getting background checks on everyone who works for you and be sure to carry liability insurance. If something unfortunate happens between a teacher and a client, you will be the one in the legal crosshairs.

My academy is now a healthy, high six-figure business—but it took a lot of work and learning to get there. You can indeed make money having teachers work for you, but be prepared to be a true boss and business owner or you can get screwed over just like I did.

A quick word on partnering with another teacher: It is very tempting to have a business partner when growing your studio, and while partnerships can be successful, there are a whole lot of ways they can go bad.

Make sure you have all responsibilities laid out on paper before proceeding, from the financial obligations to the operational duties of running the business. You should also lay out the exit strategy in case one of you wants to leave or you want to dissolve the entire enterprise.

We all have relationships in our lives that started out great only to go sour in ways we couldn't have imagined—and the ending of business partnerships are often worse than personal relationships, with animosity, hurt feelings, and lost money.

I have been in a couple of partnerships in my career, and I am MUCH happier running my own business.

Even if your prospective partner is a close friend, be REALLY careful when considering a partnership—in fact, be even more careful if the two of you are close!

Events

Events are another possible profit channel. I have been a guest speaker at many events and masterclasses, but I have not put one on myself. I have seen teachers do well financially with events, but they are also a financial risk.

I would suggest starting with very small events in order to minimize your potential downside.

Of your possible revenue sources, the ones with the smallest capital outlay and risk are the online product, followed by a book. Expanding to employees and events are something I recommend doing later when you are really getting established.

The book and product nicely dovetail into each other and can help each other grow. The book creates authority and drives traffic to your product, which is then more likely to be purchased because the customer already knows how awesome you are from reading your epic masterpiece.

If you do go forward with an event, you should absolutely capture everything on video. Spend the money to hire a small crew to do this. You don't need top-notch professionals; local students would be able to do a fine job. At the very least get a camera on a tripod and turn it on!

These videos can become a future product or even bonuses to help sell a product. Small portions of the event can be free content on your site to help drive traffic and awareness. It is also a great way to sell to those who wanted to attend but could not afford it.

Courses

This is my favorite source of additional revenue because once you build the machine, it becomes a passive source of additional income. Also, the authority and student stream you will get from a well-made and well-marketed singing information course will raise your income levels on the teaching side as well.

I currently offer courses on voice science, belt singing, as well as in-depth training to become a contemporary voice teacher. Each of these is a combination of audio, video, and downloadable slides and transcriptions.

A course is not low-hanging fruit. There is a learning curve not only in the creation of the content, but in the technology of delivering your course to the consumer, as well as selling your course.

Luckily, there are now options that make everything easier, but they are also more expensive. It will ultimately depend on how much you want to save versus how much technology you want to deal with.

I built my first course on Wordpress, which is a wonderful platform for building websites but takes a bit more work to set up the product delivery.

In order for you to sell your course, a number of things need to happen. You need a payment system to collect the money and disperse it to you. This system needs to be connected to a shopping cart, which is the interface the customer uses to purchase your course. This cart needs to be secure to protect the consumer's financial information.

Next, the course itself needs to be password-protected to prevent it from being accessed by those who have not paid for it. This password system needs to automatically and immediately send the login information to new purchasers. This is done through membership protection software. This software often (but not always) includes the above-mentioned shopping cart.

An email autoresponder is also necessary. It will send out not just important information about your course, but it will be a big part of your marketing system. You will also need to house your videos on a protected server so they cannot be accessed without payment.

Wordpress is free, but your product themes and tools listed above will all cost a monthly fee. Also, when Wordpress updates, some of these products may no longer work together, causing all sorts of headaches. After my first WordPress experience, I started to scour the world of all-in-one solutions.

These platforms provide all of the above solutions for one single payment. The main advantage is all of the elements work together nearly flawlessly because they are housed under the same development roof. This is in contrast to Wordpress, where you are dealing with plug-ins and elements from different developers that can, at times, conflict with each other and derail your site (a nightmare I don't want you to experience).

While these all-in-one systems have an initial higher monthly price than getting started with Wordpress, I have found they ultimately save me money and, more importantly, time and frustration. Remember, through all of this, you need to place a monetary value on your time (I recommend at least $200 per hour). Do not get bogged down in low-value work.

I currently use KAJABI for all of my course delivery. It provides everything I need for course creation, housing, and marketing. I have compiled a list of tools and links for readers of this book at johnhenny. com/bookbonusNow let's look at how to create your amazing product!

Chapter Fifteen
COURSE CREATION

Imagine waking up in the morning to find you have earned more income overnight than you would have in a full day's teaching. Online courses are the single best source of passive income and one successful course can change your financial life.

The good news is it is easier than ever to create online courses. Your smartphone likely has a camera that works well enough for our needs. A decent mic, some inexpensive lights, perhaps a backdrop, and we are ready to roll video!

You might be thinking the idea of getting on camera is terrifying, but I want you to get out of this mindset as quickly as possible. You don't need to be slick or a supermodel. The people who want (and need) to learn from you just want … you. Natural and unguarded, giving them vital information that will help them on their singing journey.

Content is king here, not production values. Of course, you don't want something out of focus with distorted sound, so there are minimal production values we need to keep—but honestly, they are indeed minimal. The YouTube and Facebook Live explosion has changed how people watch video and what they expect from it. As long as you help them learn, they will be happy.

First, we need to figure out what it is you are going to create. This is where the most common mistake is made: teachers often want to grab for the largest audience, so they pick a subject that will attract the most singers possible. I would advise against this, at least in the beginning.

"There are riches in niches." This mantra is repeated over and over by those in the online education industry. This means the more you focus down, the better chances you have of success.

Take this book you are reading. If I had written it as business tips for coaches of all kinds, you might not have picked it up and started reading. I made the decision to target voice teachers specifically because I know your language and challenges, and I can speak directly to you.

Now, is a portion of this information applicable to other coaching businesses? Certainly. But my focus on the voice teacher makes you more likely to want to purchase and consume my various products. By niching down, I have captured your attention and built your trust (hopefully!).

This is what I want you to do when creating your product. Niche down.

Is it possible to over-narrow your niche? Yes. If I had gone after voice teachers who are 6'7" tall and like bulldogs and poker, I probably would have one reader—me.

As you start the process of zeroing in on your niche, there are a few ways to test if your idea has legs.

First off, ask yourself if there is any competition in your niche. Why? Because competition is a good thing. It tells you there is interest in the topic.

If you choose a niche that has zero competition, that may be a red flag that there is little to no money to be made there.

You don't need to worry if there are already courses that teach your chosen niche—YOU are the magic ingredient the competition does not have. Your way of teaching and connecting with YOUR audience is what makes you valuable.

You can also join Facebook groups or read through forums such as Reddit to see the problems your audience wants to solve.

Create a Test Version

Before you dive into creating your magnum opus of 50 videos and worksheets, I suggest you first make and sell the smallest, quickest version of your course.

I did this recently in order to test response and interest in a course on Belting.

Rather than creating a full-length course, I made a smaller version that focuses on the science and acoustics of healthy belting—an in-depth look at how belt works. I put it together in about a day.

I put the course on sale for just $10 to gauge interest, and I quickly sold over $1,000, which told me there is an audience for a bigger, more in-depth course.

There is nothing worse than putting a lot of time into a course and finding out the interest is extremely low or non-existent. The fact that your course has information people NEED does not mean it's information they WANT.

I find that there are a number of voice teachers whose piano skills are lacking, so I created a course to help them learn how to play quickly and be able to accompany their students on a basic level.

I put the course out there expecting teachers to flock to it … and … crickets. I did not test or even survey my audience to see if it was something they wanted. Turns out, it's a hard sell—even though I think it's a great product!

Test first, and then build your bigger course.

Outline Your Course

You will want to create a detailed outline that breaks down each main subject and subsequent lessons within.

I then suggest creating a PowerPoint lecture for each lesson, from which you will then film yourself lecturing. ScreenFlow for Mac or Camtasia for Windows are programs that will record both your camera and the slides from your desktop, combining them into an effective instructional video.

I do not recommend scripting exactly what you are going to say unless you are an extremely good writer and a natural at delivering written content. You risk coming off as over-stiff, which you do not want to do. It is much better to have some flubs. I will sometimes joke about a mistake and leave it in.

The key is to be yourself and teach as if the person were sitting in your studio with you. You don't prescript what you are going to say to a student, although as a conscientious teacher you have likely given some forethought as to what you want to cover in the lesson. The PowerPoint will do this for you, keeping you on track while allowing you to converse naturally.

I would break each lesson into easy-to-consume segments, even if it means breaking a single lesson into multiple parts. Opening up a 30-minute video lesson can be daunting for students, but getting through three 10-minute videos is a breeze. Finishing a video lesson will give them a sense of accomplishment, and the momentum will move them on to the next one.

I then pull up my PowerPoint (or Keynote) presentation and begin recording with Screenflow. This not only records the presentation and audio, but I also have the option of my computer's camera capturing video of me as I speak. I have found this to work well, and many users have told me they appreciate being able to see me as I teach, but you do not have to utilize this.

I use a USB plugin mic for enhanced audio quality, which I recommend. Again, people expect better audio quality over video quality, so the extra investment is worth it. Your computer mic will tend to be distractingly poor.

My products usually consist of introductions shot in front of a backdrop, with me explaining what is to come, and then each lesson is a PowerPoint lecture with video of my computer screen. Simple, easy, and effective.

You can even outsource the editing of your videos inexpensively with services such as Fiverr and Upwork. I discuss this further in the chapter on Outsourcing.

I would suggest keeping your first product not just niche-focused, but also on the smaller side. Don't worry about not being able to charge enough because the course is shorter. You will be pricing on value, not course length.

The one mistake I made with one of my earlier courses was making it too big and unwieldy. It caused problems for me on the content side, and it was intimidating for the consumer to try to get through all those hours of lessons.

If you have a subject matter that requires a very in-depth course, consider breaking it down into multiple courses. Make what you have to teach approachable and easy-to-consume. This book is a perfect example. I could pick a number of these chapters and write many thousands of words on just that subject, but the chances of overwhelm would increase and the likelihood of you finishing the book would diminish. Instead, I am giving you the meat of each subject so you can begin to consider if it's the right course for you.

Remember, you will get better at course creation, just as your students get better at singing. Their first performance will not be as good as their 10th, and your courses will improve as you create them. What I love about the online medium is being able to go back and change anything at any time. Updating your content is also a great way to keep current users happy and coming back.

The Recurring Revenue Model

Once you have a product or two under your belt, start thinking about creating a membership site with a monthly payment structure. Having consistent monthly income is where you can make truly positive changes in your teaching life.

I currently have two subscription sites. The first is my Contemporary Voice Teacher Academy (CVTA), where I train people from the very beginning (some never having taught a lesson) to become solid, successful voice teachers.

My second subscription product is CVTA Elite. This course is an upsell from the CVTA for experienced teachers who want more one-on-one contact and training with me. In CVTA Elite, I will critique videos of them teaching, as well as teach their students as they observe. I also provide personal business coaching to help teachers grow their reach and business.

Both of these sites provide me with a consistent revenue stream, which is harder to do with stand-alone courses.

As you create, test, and publish courses, you will start to build content for a membership site. You will also get valuable feedback as to what your audience most wants to learn from you. I suggest starting with a few smaller courses and then building up to the monthly membership model.

I have created a list of my favorite course creation tools in the member's area of this book: johnhenny.com/bookbonus

Online courses are inexpensive to produce and deliver and can ultimately become a foundation of your business and income.

Chapter Sixteen

MARKETING

Embracing The Ugly Truth

Art is beautiful. It is a world of expression, love, joy, and the promise of perfection. Business, on the other hand, is anything but. It thrives on cold, blunt realities in which we need to face the hard truths and do the not-always-fun work. Now there are jobs you can delegate, and jobs you should not. One of the key mistakes I see voice teachers make as their business grows is hiding from jobs they don't enjoy—and one of these key jobs is marketing.

Marketing is the one job you do not want to outsource in the beginning. Why? Because you need to have a good working knowledge of the process. This is because marketing can get wasteful and expensive in a hurry, and then the temptation is to throw it away completely because it doesn't work. This will take the gas out of your growth engine.

I have also seen voice teachers (I will assume this is not you) who dismiss marketing skills as "easy" and beneath them. This is a huge mistake. Marketing is a skill set with as much nuance and depth as the voice. Like singing, it can take many years to master. While you don't need to become a super copywriter or a Facebook ad expert, you should still learn the basics thoroughly.

The Marketing Funnel

Here's where we begin to put the pieces into motion and create your marketing strategy. You do not need to (and probably shouldn't attempt to) do everything at once. This is indeed a marathon, and you will be refining and improving your marketing for as long as you are in business.

Each part of your marketing should help amplify and tie into the next step, leading the potential customer through your marketing journey so when they reach the end, they are happy to either recommend you enthusiastically or become a client themselves.

Sales Funnel

The sales funnel concept is the way most marketers view their customer journey, and they adjust their advertising message to speak to the customer at whichever stage of the funnel they find themselves.

The three main parts of the funnel are: Top of Funnel, Middle of Funnel, and Bottom of Funnel.

Here's how it works:

Sales Funnel

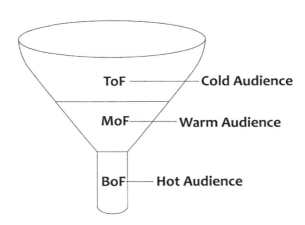

You will notice the top of the funnel (TOF) is larger and wider than the middle (MOF), which is wider than the bottom (BOF). This is because as people go through your funnel there will be less and less of them that get to the bottom (often dramatically less), and this is a good thing!

Why would we want less and less people? Because the job of the funnel is to sift through a large number of people and identify those who want to buy from you, and from that group, those who REALLY want to buy from you: the SUPER BUYER.

Think of something you are absolutely passionate about, to the point where you will buy anything and everything related to it.

I happen to love coffee, and I am sipping a big beautiful mug of it as I type this. Now, this is not coffee I purchased at my local Starbucks. No, it is coffee I roasted myself in a roasting machine, from green beans sourced online, and brewed in a coffee maker so precise I can control the water temperature from my phone.

I am a super-buyer of all things coffee. And I have friends who are much more super-crazy than I am—we're talking purchasing $10,000 espresso machines! Now, you may think we are bonkers, but there is likely a similar passion in your life.

You will also have super buyers who are superfans of what you do. There are two things you want to do: identify who they are and create premium offerings to sell to them.

The funnel will help you identify your super buyers, as well as the larger group of customers who, while not necessarily buying your most expensive offerings, will purchase your less expensive products and lessons but in greater number.

One key point is to always consider the customer's mindset as they go through your funnel and speak to them where they are. You do not want to speak to the TOF the same as you would the MOF. They are at different places in the decision-making process.

Audiences

Audience types are going to closely relate to the funnel, but it is worth a deeper look at each type and how they should be approached.

There are three main types of audiences most marketers consider: Cold, Warm, and Hot. Each of these temperatures refers to where they are in relation to you and your funnel, and each level will require their own special treatment as they move through the funnel.

Cold Audience

Cold audiences are the largest group and they are the lifeblood of attracting new business. The cold audience is people who have not heard of you. They may not even be aware they have a problem to be solved. How you approach this audience will depend on your avatar and preferred client. It's always important to know to whom you are talking.

If you teach classical singers, you exist in a culture that is very solution-aware. Among this group, it is an aberration *not* to take voice lessons. Your cold audience just needs to be made aware that you are the solution to problems they are seeking answers to.

If you work with a lot of singer-songwriter types, voice lessons are not necessarily top of mind. They might not be aware of potential problems down the vocal road, so you may need to make them problem-aware, and then solution-aware.

Whichever type of singer you are going after, they will initially be a cold audience so we will need to cast a wide net. Most of them will never go further on this journey with you, which is fine. We are looking to get those who are a good fit for you to raise their hand and move on to the next part of the journey.

Cold audiences are TOF (top of funnel), and you will use TOF materials to grab their attention. Asking a cold audience for a sale is usually a mistake (unless it is a specific low-priced offer that's easy for them to say "yes" to). You want to start the relationship by providing value, and that's why we make specific TOF material.

What we want is to get the cold audience member to consume some piece of useful content, to establish awareness of you and your authority, before moving onto the next phase.

Cold audience material will be blog posts, podcasts, video tips, etc. We want the cold audience to consume some type of helpful information from you, which will then put you on their radar. And hopefully they will want to consume more of your content.

This moves us into the warm audience category.

Warm Audience

The warm audience is comprised of people who have now read, watched, or interacted with you and your content in some manner. They will be far fewer in number than the cold audience, but much more likely to want to work with you.

This is where you want to make some sort of offer. It can be a free consultation, an initial lesson, a low-priced eBook or short video course—anything that makes them take action. This will create momentum in the buying process.

If you have an online course, the typical audience/funnel strategy is to drive traffic (cold audience) to content, then make an offer for a lead magnet, which is something of value in exchange for an email address. Getting the email address is a key step for the potential client as they are now taking a small step of trust in you. They are taking action.

The next step is a low-dollar offer, usually between $5 to $20. This is often called a trip-wire (as we mentioned earlier, what a horrible name!) as it sets off the buying process. Even as little as $5 has created a dynamic shift in the relationship and turned this person into a buyer, setting them up to make larger purchases in the future.

Once they have purchased from you, even a small amount, they become part of your hot audience.

Hot Audience

No, these are not your best-looking potential clients, these are the people who have raised their hands and said they want to buy from you. These are extremely important people.

Now, if someone doesn't move to this part of the funnel/audience journey and stays warm for a while, that's OK. People often take a while to convert, and we don't want to give up on them.

The hot audience people are the ones who will receive the BOF (bottom of funnel) content. You will continue to provide value, but you will also create ways for them to get more access to you, whether it's special products, webinars, or one-to-one access.

A mistake many teachers make at this stage is not asking for the sale. It's like watching a romantic comedy where the sweet, shy guy can't get up the courage to ask the clearly interested girl out on a date. Don't be that guy!

If you have provided valuable content, and a portion of your audience has shown this level of interest, then make them an offer! Don't be afraid of asking them to purchase higher-ticket items.

But be cautious! You can easily take this too far and become the pushy used car dealer. You need to strike a balance between continually providing solid helpful content and asking for sales.

The key takeaway here is to not approach one segment of your audience like another. If you make high-ticket offers right away to a cold audience, you will likely chase a number of them away, never to return. If you don't make offers to your warm and hot audiences, you won't make money!

Now we come to the next part… What do you say to these prospective clients at each level of the funnel?

Chapter Seventeen
COPYWRITING

Copywriting is the art of persuasion. It is all about taking someone through the journey from being introduced to you all the way to buying your offerings.

Copywriting is a high-level skill, and those at the top of the profession can get paid hundreds of thousands of dollars, plus a percentage of the profits, for just one sales letter.

But no need to worry, we certainly don't need to hire anyone that expensive. I actually encourage you to begin writing your own copy, ads, marketing emails, and sales pages, because no one knows your audience like you do.

Even if you choose to have someone else eventually do your copywriting, I suggest you at least get familiar with these fundamentals and spend some time learning them. These basic skills will help you guide whoever you hire to do the best job possible talking to your audience.

You will be able to talk to and connect with your audience (and avatar) in the right way as long as you keep them front-of-mind.

I heard bestselling author James Patterson talk about his approach to writing a book. He said he simply imagines someone sitting in front of him and telling this person a story. Patterson's goal is that he does not want the person to get up and leave. He imagines keeping the listener riveted the entire time.

This approach is very instructional for our needs. If we write so the potential client doesn't want to stop listening, we have a very good chance of making a sale.

While this is in no way a complete course on copywriting (that could fill another very large book), these concepts will give you some of the essential basics and will instantly increase customer interaction with your website, ads, and emails.

Benefits Not Features

When we have a product or offer lessons, it is always tempting to talk about what interests us and the work we have put into it. But just as we discussed earlier, all of our messaging needs to be 100% focused on the potential client. And clients want to know about the benefits, not the features.

What is the difference between a benefit and a feature? A feature is what you are offering, while a benefit is what the student will gain from the offering.

For example: you offer lessons in a high-density area so you soundproofed your studio. You then list on your website "soundproof lesson room." That is a feature. But what is the benefit?

A benefit would be "take your voice lessons in a completely private environment without worrying about others hearing you." The feature is the soundproofing, but the benefit is the privacy it affords the student.

If you have an online course you might want to offer audio downloads of each lesson. This, again, is a feature.

What is the benefit? The ability to listen to your lessons in the car or while exercising.

The benefits are all about the client, and benefits are going to have the most impact on them. Keep the client top-of-mind—they are sitting at your kitchen table and you are talking directly to them. Don't let them get up and leave.

Lingo

As voice teachers, we all have buzzwords we use so much we don't think about whether people understand them. Chest voice, vocal fry, twang, passagio, mixed voice, pedagogy, etc.

Many of these terms may be unfamiliar to your particular audience, however, especially if you are dealing with beginners or parents. Always be mindful of being completely clear and keeping your ideas simple and easy-to-understand.

I once wrote an article for *Backstage Magazine* where I interviewed the voice teacher of a famous artist. A friend alerted me there was an online discussion about my article by the artist's fans.

Even though most of them enjoyed the article, some talked about how they struggled to understand some of the jargon. While the article was written for a more professional or experienced reader, I thought I had kept it simple enough for the average person to understand. I was obviously wrong.

People can get easily confused, especially online where they scan the material incredibly quickly. By keeping your copy clear and jargon-free, you will be better able to attract and hold your audience's attention.

They Are the Star Of the Show

I will keep hammering this home: it's not about you. Your potential client is the star of their story, and you cannot compete with their top billing. You must play a critical, secondary role.

Don Miller, the creator of StoryBrand method of copywriting, talks about you being the guide to their hero, or the Obi Wan to their Luke Skywalker.

You must allow the client to take center stage in this dialogue and be there to support and guide them. You will play an essential role, but not the central one.

Make everything about the hero's needs, fears, and desires, and then show how you are the wise guide to help them through the obstacles and on to success. Do this, and you will be rewarded with a steady stream of clients. Let this inform everything you write and communicate in your business.

Easy to Read

People don't read online, they scan. Keep your paragraphs short and your language simple and to the point. This means no more than two or three sentences per paragraph.

You should also have sub-headlines to break up the flow and reestablish copy points. This gives the reader an opportunity to stop scanning and read a little deeper if a point is of more interest to them.

If you are making a new point, create a new sub-headline. For instance, if your audition techniques class will also help them prepare their music, create a sub-headline like:

Don't Make These Mistakes with Your Sheet Music

This will grab the reader's attention and get them to refocus on your message, especially if they've ever had an issue with their music and dealing with a cranky accompanist (another great topic!).

Bullet points are also a great way to format for scanning. Why is this?

- Easy to read
- Focuses attention
- Great for making strong points
- Breaks up the visual flow

Testimonials

Testimonials are the ultimate social proof and should be featured prominently in your advertising, copy, and website.

The issue for many voice teachers is that it can feel awkward to ask for testimonials. Here are a couple of ways to do it.

There are times during lessons where a student will spontaneously give you a compliment or comment that would work great as a testimonial, usually when they have experienced a breakthrough. When the student says something like, "I've never been able to sing this high with this much freedom," you can say, "Thank you, I really appreciate the kind words. Would you mind if I used this as a testimonial?"

I have been asked numerous times for a testimonial and I am always flattered. The idea that someone you respect and are learning from values your opinion enough to share with others is almost always received in a positive manner.

You can also ask a satisfied student to hop on a quick Skype call to answer a few questions. Ask them what problems they were dealing with and how your lessons helped them overcome them. Every prospective client wants to know how you can help them solve a problem—so give them proof!

The PAS Formula

There are many different approaches to advertising and writing copy, but one incredibly popular and effective formula is Problem, Agitate, Solution, or PAS.

By using the PAS formula as the basis for your copy, you will be able to lay out your case as to why someone should study with or buy from you. This will help motivate them to take action, especially if you are tuned in to your customer avatar and writing directly to them.

Here's the way it works: First, we identify a problem; the more specific to your avatar the better. The problem should also be specific to the solution you wish to sell—and everything we sell is a solution to a problem.

For example: if your audience is musical theatre performers, you can focus on the embarrassment of a poor audition.

A typical headline could be: *Was Your Last Audition a Disaster?*

Then you can dive into and agitate the problem more. We want the reader to feel an emotional response, to really experience and remember why they need to solve and eliminate this problem from happening again.

We can then continue: *You knew you were perfect for the role, you felt prepared and ready, and yet everything fell apart when you started singing. That awful feeling of walking out of the audition knowing you could have done so much better.*

At this point the reader is likely worked up, especially if singing is incredibly important to them. Now we need to offer a solution, showing them that we, as the wise guide, can change their story into a happy one.

Now is a good time for a little self-promotion, but again, the focus is on how your experience can help *them*. It's not about you, it's about how you have helped others like them.

As a voice teacher I have helped hundreds of singers learn to nail their auditions and get the role. Get the specific skills you need to confidently walk into the audition room every time and deliver your best.

The PAS formula is one you will see again and again because it works. It is simple, direct, and emotionally effective. Most decisions are made on emotion and then later justified with logic. By appealing to the reader's emotions of frustration and embarrassment, and then providing the solution, you provide a strong emotional cue that you are the person who can end the pain they are experiencing.

The deeper the pain point, the more likely they are to make the choice to have you solve it.

What Do You Have?

They have a problem, you have further agitated them about this problem, so they are seeking relief. You have told them you are the solution to this problem, so now let them know what you have that will fix said problem: Your masterclass, lessons, online program, book, etc.

Remember, focus on the benefits not the features of your product or lessons.

Rather than "You get 20 video lessons and a workbook," you might say "20 lessons that build your skills and confidence step-by-step, along with a workbook of powerful techniques that will make you unstoppable at your next audition."

Don't just tell them what they will get, tell them what it will do for them. Tell them how will it solve the problem.

Tell Them What To Do

This is the point where many voice teachers drop the ball. They don't tell the client exactly what they need to do. Don't expect people to be mind-readers or to take the next step without a little prompting.

You've got them ready to solve their problem, now tell them the exact steps they need to take to get the solution. Tell them what you have and how to get it!

Click here to access my free Audition Tips video series.

Call now to schedule your appointment.

Enter your contact information below and my staff will get back to you shortly.

Always be thinking of the client. Consider their mindset, their hesitations to buying, and the constant onslaught of online distractions they face. By making explicit instructions, you make them have to think less, and thinking less is a huge key to the process.

Have you ever purchased something from Amazon knowing you are likely overpaying a little? I know I have, but what I get in return is the ease of the transaction. I don't have to think about the process, and I relish moments of rest for this little brain of mine.

What Will Life Be Like After?

One of the primary goals of good copy is to put the client in the idealized state of "after," or what their life will be like when they solve this problem.

We all think our lives would be so much better if we could only have X. By going into the mental picture of this ideal life, we yearn for it all the more. Reminding the client of this state can be a powerful nudge.

Get my Audition Course and Let Them See Your True Talent.

You can also let the client know what life might be like if they *don't* get your course. This one is a bit negative, so you want to be careful how you use it. You will reinforce the problem and tie it back to the client not taking action, not buying your course, or not making an appointment.

I usually keep this a bit subtle, as I don't want to browbeat the client as I am making the pitch for action. I might amend the above line this way:

End the Frustration of Failed Auditions, Get My Audition Course and Let Your True Talent Shine Through.

I have now included a little reminder as to what the future will be without taking action: more of the same misery of failed auditions. Putting the two potential futures side-by-side in the client's mind paints a powerful mental picture and can drive them to take the action you are asking for.

Use Your Powers For Good

I am well aware that this copywriting stuff sounds a bit cynical, a bit like mind control, and it is. Many of these techniques go back over 100 years and are almost unchanged.

What was used in newspapers in the early 1900s was later used in radio, then TV infomercials, and now on webinars and Facebook.

We humans are surrounded by more and more technology, yet we are essentially the same creatures, with the same needs of acceptance and fears of rejection. Advertisers capitalize on this.

These advertising techniques are also used by the unscrupulous to con and defraud others, but they are also used by very good people and companies to bring products and services to those who would very much benefit from them.

You are one of the good people. As a fellow educator, I know your heart and your desire to help others. You have a wealth of experience and knowledge that can help others achieve their goals and dreams—the problem is they are being bombarded by junk they don't need, junk that is fighting for their attention, time, and budget.

You owe it to them to get your message front and center and to convince them (through all of their built-up resistance and suspicion) to trust you and your instruction. The truth is your product or lessons can help people, people who really need it, so keeping yourself too humble or too afraid to put you (and your marketing) out there deprives this person of getting the unique help that only you can provide.

We, as voice teachers, often feel uncomfortable when it comes to this kind of marketing. Simply listing our education or affiliations as our "sales pitch" feels proper—it feels safe and non-salesy. Proper and effective copywriting can feel anything but that, especially at first, but this is where you have an amazing opportunity.

The human decision-making process is not always pretty, and it certainly is not always right. By embracing effective copywriting and honest marketing, you are embracing the truth of the human condition and our need to be convinced on an emotional level.

"But I hate this type of selling!" you might say, but you need to remember it's about your client, not you. You are in the business of teaching voice, and you have a unique perspective that the general public does not have. You cannot expect, nor should you make the mistake of expecting, your potential students to view your marketing through your eyes.

Market in an honest yet effective way, and you will soon be able to reach beyond your studio to impact singers' lives around the world, if you so choose.

Chapter Eighteen
YOUR EMAIL LIST

Your email list can be your single greatest marketing asset for one simple reason: it's yours and it costs you nothing to use it whenever you want.

While Facebook/Instagram ads and Google Ad Words are the fastest and easiest way to get the ball rolling, they do have some disadvantages.

The first is cost. They can get a bit expensive, especially if you don't set them up correctly, which can be a big investment in time and money in and of itself.

But more than that, the lists you build on these platforms belong to them, and you lose access to them if your account is ever closed down.

Your email list, however, is yours to keep forever. Beyond the monthly fee to your email service provider, there are no additional charges each time you use it to market your products and services.

The downside is email lists take significant work and time to build. You can be in front of tens of thousands of people in your local area on Facebook today, but it could take many months or years to get this kind of reach with your email list.

It is still well worth your while to begin to build your list; it's just a longer game than paid advertising.

There are a few key mistakes I want you to avoid:

1. Don't try and run your list from a free account such as Gmail. Spam catchers will tend to flag marketing emails coming from a Gmail account, resulting in your beautifully constructed marketing poetry going straight to the spam folder.

You will want to use a service specifically designed to send large numbers of email. These services are not very expensive at first, but the costs will grow as your list grows.

Mail Chimp is a popular service that can accomplish this for you, and has a free tier which is perfect for starting out.

2. Offering a newsletter to sign up. People are stingier with their email addresses these days, and the vague promise of a newsletter doesn't work so well anymore.

As I pointed out in the Sales Funnel chapter, we need a specific piece of content to get people to opt-in and share their email address. This should be a special piece of content that goes more in-depth than a blog post.

You can also offer lists, such as the best open mics in your area or your favorite singing videos. You can do a short eBook or a video series. Just be sure to solve a problem your audience is likely experiencing.

My music academy offers a "Parent's Guide to Music Lessons" eBook in exchange for an email address.

3. Not emailing your list regularly. This will be a bit hard at first, and this is where most teachers suffer from fatigue and tap out. Your list needs to hear from you on a regular basis, not just when you have something to sell.

Interesting, engaging emails from you will keep your list excited and looking forward to hearing from you.

The best way to write your emails is in your authentic voice. Don't worry about precise grammar or $5 words (unless your audience is academics). You don't want misspelled words or atrocious grammar, of course, but you also don't want to come across stiff and stilted.

The goal of the emails is to get people to learn more about you and how you approach the craft of singing. You will not be the right fit for everyone, so our goal in all of our marketing is to get people to raise their heads and say, "Yes, you are the right teacher for me."

The more they get the true you, the more likely they are going to think you're the one.

Types of Emails

There are two basic types of email you will want to use: autoresponse (or automatic) and broadcast.

Autoresponse emails are prewritten and sent automatically when the prospective client hits a certain trigger, such as signing up for your list. They will then receive a batch of prewritten emails over a series of days or weeks.

These emails are usually used to introduce the reader to you, talk about what you can provide, and show how you can solve their problems.

Typical emails in this sequence will be an initial welcome and thank you for signing up to your list, as well as letting the reader know what to expect from you in the upcoming weeks and months.

It's also a good idea to have an email directing them to some of your best or most popular content, whether it's a blog post, video, podcast episode, etc.

We do not want autoresponse emails to be our only mode of communication, though, as they can quickly get stale and not feel authentic. This is where broadcast emails come in.

A broadcast email is much more like how you likely think of email today—it's written once and consumed once, basically in real time.

These emails are the ones you will be writing on a regular basis, as opposed to the automatic emails, which are more set-and-forget type deals.

The broadcast email is where you create more of a connection with your subscribers. Since they are often written and sent in the same day, you can talk about current events or what is going on in your particular musical world.

Current events are not a good idea for auto emails, as we want these to be evergreen, and references to events would make them appear dated very quickly.

You can talk about the Grammys, the Tony Awards, Metropolitan Opera Auditions, the hit song of the week, anything music-related that connects with your particular audience.

I also find popular culture in general to be a great topic starter. This can be a popular movie, Netflix series, etc. All of this will make your emails seem current and relevant.

You should also tell stories about yourself, your students, their wins, and what you're excited about right now. This will make you more personable and relatable.

The key to broadcast emails is to be consistent with them. You don't need to email every day—although you could if you are an inspired enough writer—but at least once a week is a good goal to shoot for.

All of the friendly chit-chat in the email should lead up to providing value for the reader. I will use the references and stories to tie into a vocal tip or a new piece of content for them to consume.

You can even link to an article or post on singing that you find interesting (people love to be linked to), but don't reproduce their content in your email without permission. The great part of linking other great content is you don't have to spend time creating new material, yet the reader will still appreciate you for sending the information their way.

I would not overdo the linking of other content, though. You need to be producing good content to create your ultimate authority in the reader's mind—besides, you want to keep sending people to *your* site.

Your emails will have a twofold effect—to make you more relatable (even enjoyable to read) and to connect you to even more value. Authority and perceived value are the one-two punch of voice teacher success. As your authority and value go up, so do your bottom line and profitability.

The Sale

Sales are always the ultimate goal of any marketing, so don't be afraid to include an offer in your emails. Often, a brief mention and link at the bottom of the email can be enough. A lot of marketers will use a PS to mention their offer, as many readers will jump down and read the PS even if they don't look at much else.

You can do emails that are completely sales-driven—these are usually reserved for when you have a brand new offer, a sale, or a special event coming up, such as a masterclass or open house.

These more blatant sales emails will be welcomed by your list as long as they are not the only type of email they get from you. Even when really pushing the sale, I would still include some humor, story, or a bit of your personality. Stay likable, never pushy or over-salesy.

Chapter Nineteen
SOCIAL MEDIA

There are a number of media channels available to you in order to grow your audience, with more coming all the time. For this book, I am going to focus on Facebook.

Why Facebook? Because it is far and away the largest of all the social media channels. Your future students and customers are on Facebook. Facebook also owns Instagram, so syncing between the two is relatively easy.

There are two basic ways you can reach customers on Facebook: through organic content and paid advertising. While organic content is free, and any exposure we can get through it is of course wonderful, I want you to pony up and pay for advertising.

Why pay when you can put your content out there for free? Because your organic content is becoming less and less effective.

Ever since Facebook became a public company, they have shifted their model to more and more paid reach. Facebook has little interest in showing people your business content for free. Also, the space in a user's timeline has become more valuable as more advertisers and users join the platform. This means you need to pay in order to engage with people who are not your close friends and family.

Can you still get viral pieces of content? Sure, but it's hard to do and you give up control as you wait for people to share your content. Plus, our material will be of specific interest to singers and not the general public, so the chances of going viral are vanishingly small.

The good news is you can advertise for just a few dollars a day—and if done right, these few dollars can have a huge impact on your business.

The Power of Facebook

As we now know from recent headlines, Facebook is in the data collection business. Facebook has so much personal information on you that they work very hard to not let you know HOW MUCH they have. They know when you are sleeping, they know when you're awake. You get the idea…

When you open your Facebook account, you are giving Mr. Zuckerberg and company an open window into your life. Every article you read, post you like, and even other websites you visit are tracked by Facebook, and all this information is then sold to advertisers. You and your personal life are a commodity.

As a private citizen, this is absolutely frightening and one of the greatest invasions of privacy ever devised. As an advertiser, it is an amazing opportunity!

Facebook's vast database allows you to pinpoint who sees your ads, right down to where they live, if they have children, if they drink coffee, if they like to go hiking, and yes, if they are interested in singing.

This gives us a golden opportunity to reach potential students in a profound and immediate way, as long as we are willing to pay for it. Part of Facebook's messaging power is that it is passive advertising.

Passive advertising is different from active, like Google, where the consumer is taking direct action to look for your services. The obvious power of active advertising is the consumer is likely ready to buy or is further down the research journey in looking for goods or services.

Passive gets to the consumer earlier, before they have really started looking for lessons. If you can get to the consumer early and make a good impression, then your chances of getting them as a client go up greatly. If you can establish yourself as the authority right away, their later research will likely be to convince themselves to go with you and not your competitors. If your message is simple, direct, and strong—and your content is helpful and easy to implement—you are well on your way to making the sale.

Facebook gives us the most powerful way to get in front of the greatest number of people.

The science and art of Facebook advertising is a vast subject, and I spend a lot of time working with teachers on it, but there are some key elements you should understand that can help get you started. Because you can advertise for as little as a few dollars a day, I recommend you take these lessons and dive in. As I tell my private marketing students, even a poor Facebook campaign works better than nothing at all.

Your Facebook Business Page

You will need your own business page. This doesn't need to be anything too fancy, but it will serve as the basis for your advertising efforts. Facebook does not want you running your business from your personal profile.

One mistake people often make is getting family and friends to like their page—I recommend against this, as you want to keep the page strictly business. Another big mistake I often see is boosting posts (i.e., paying Facebook to show your post to people who like your page), which then goes out to a bunch of friends and family. While your Uncle Ted may be somewhat lovable (even if he drinks too much at Christmas), having him jumping on your posts with bad puns is not going to help your cause. He's not going to buy lessons, and it costs you money to have your ad appear in his Facebook feed. Save your Uncle Ted for family get-togethers, and please keep him away from the bourbon.

Boosting a post is basically Facebook's gateway to get you to start spending money. They make it very simple—just press a button, and as easy as that, you've given them some cash and you're advertising.

The problem is your post is likely not going to the right people with the right message. It also might not have the correct objective. Let's take a moment to break this down.

Facebook Objectives

Each ad you run on Facebook will have a specific objective. These objectives can be for people to interact with your post (get likes), to have them click on a link in your ad, to have them watch a video, to download your app, and so on.

This means Facebook studies the behavior of its users and will show your ad to those most likely to take the action you are looking for. If you want people to click on a link to your musical theatre auditioning class, but the objective chosen is Engagement, Facebook will show the ad to people who will click "like" or comment, but not to those who tend to click on links and get further information.

While getting "likes" always feels good, it does not feel as good as making a sale. We want potential buyers, the ones who like to take action and do things, to see our ads.

The main objectives we will want to use are Clicks to Website and Video Views. Clicking to our site is a great way to show our content, make sales, and build audiences. Video Views are a fantastic way to build your audience and build awareness. Video is becoming a larger part of my overall advertising strategy.

As we discussed in the chapter on video, creating a video ad is simple. All you need is your smartphone and a plugin lapel mic to make sure your sound is good.

The absolute key to video ads is subtitles or captions. Most ads are watched in the scroll with the sound off, so you don't want to force the viewer to have to turn up the volume to get your message—after all, they may not be in a place they want to have volume spilling out, such as an elevator, bank line, etc.

Luckily, Facebook has made this easy for us by offering auto-captioning. This is a huge timesaver and very easy to utilize. I have made a video showing you how it works:

johnhenny.com/bookbonus

Clicks to Website is my preferred objective. This tells Facebook to show my ad to people who are likely to take action and click the link in the ad. This link will go either to specific content, such as a useful blog post or to a landing page with a specific offer and call to action, depending on the type of audience (cold or warm).

Be aware that Facebook is a constantly growing and evolving medium, so they are changing the interface all the time. The names of objectives, or the buttons you press to get to them, may at some point be different from what they are referred to in this book, but the basic interactions remain the same. We are looking for people who will take action and are likely to utilize our services. Keep that in mind and you will know what to use, regardless of what Facebook currently calls it.

The Facebook Pixel

I tell everyone who takes one of my marketing courses that if they get no other piece of information from me, if they take no other action, they at least need to get their pixel working.

What is the Facebook pixel? It is a piece of code, unique to you, that you put on your website or landing pages. It is invisible to the visitor and works in the background, alerting Facebook when someone has visited your website.

When alerted, Facebook then places the visitor into an "audience," a grouping of everyone who visits your site. Why is this important? Because most visitors will leave your site without taking any further action. They won't give up their email address, and they won't contact you for further information.

This does not necessarily mean they are not interested; they are likely very interested because they took the time and action to visit your site. They are just victims of the online ADD that we all suffer from.

Online distractions, as well as real-life ones, are constant, and the interested person may get called away from your page by a phone call at home or a meeting at work. Perhaps they have jumped from your site to a competitor's as they research potential voice teachers. Once gone and distracted, they often don't find their way back.

The pixel solves this by collecting all of these visitors and setting them aside as an audience to be "retargeted" or reminded at a later time.

This audience is an extremely valuable asset as it is made up exclusively of people who have visited your site or interacted with your content. This is a "warm audience" made up of people who are much more likely to buy from you than a cold audience.

You can then utilize this audience in different ways by breaking it down further for advertising purposes.

I have a couple of very popular blog posts on my website that get a lot of traffic. When a reader visits my blog, my pixel informs Facebook and they are placed in an audience. I then can run ads to this audience, but I don't always want to use everyone in this pixel group. Why?

Because this audience is often larger, it has people in it I don't always want to target.

For example, if I am running ads for an upcoming masterclass at my studio, I only want to target people within a certain geographic range. While the idea of someone traveling thousands of miles for one of my masterclasses is a nice ego boost, it is very unlikely to happen.

I am then able to take my large audience of pixeled website visitors and pare it down to people within a certain mile radius of my studio. Because I am in a large, congested metropolitan area (the traffic nightmare that is Los Angeles), my radius would be smaller than someone in a beautiful, open, spacious, low-crime, affordable area (sigh).

Another reason to separate my pixeled audience is by the page they visited. If I have a post on the best vocal tips when recording a demo versus a post on auditioning for college, I likely don't want to run an ad for a recording masterclass to people who visited my auditioning post. However, if I am running a more generalized ad for vocal lessons, I would include both sets of visitors.

The pixel not only lets you run ads to an audience of people who already know who you are, but it allows you to break them down in very specific ways. Every day you do not have the pixel on your site, you are allowing potential students to wander away, never to be seen again.

The good news is the pixel is not only free but easy to install, with a bit of technical know-how. You also have the option of having Facebook email all of the pixel info to your webmaster, who can install it in just a few minutes. I have included a video on installing the pixel in the member's area at johnhenny.com/bookbonus

Facebook Audiences

Understanding your audiences is key to running effective Facebook ads. They are your number one Facebook asset, and there are a few main types of audiences you can build.

Custom Audience

This audience is made up of people who have interacted with you. They may have been pixeled, have watched your videos on Facebook, or have been uploaded from your customer lists.

If you have an email list of past clients, you can also upload them into Facebook and Facebook will find them for you. This is perfect for running a win-back campaign telling past clients how much they are missed and inviting them back to your studio.

The Custom Audience is always a warm or hot audience and extremely valuable to you. You want to be constantly building these audiences as part of your marketing strategy.

The advertising concept here is called "retargeting," and it is the secret weapon of successful businesses.

For example, have you ever looked at a website for a particular product, only to have this product now follow you around the internet? This is retargeting.

I am currently in the market for high-quality wireless headphones. I have looked at a number of brands, but one in particular keeps showing up in my Facebook and Instagram feeds, reminding me why their headphones are the best solution for my listening needs.

If a potential client has visited your website along with three of your competitors, but you are the one reappearing in their Facebook feed reminding them why YOU are the solution to their vocal problems, you have an incredible advantage over your less-savvy competitors.

Saved Audience

This audience is made up of people who are likely not aware of you, but with one huge difference from the general public: they have interests that make them likely to want to know more about your services.

You will create your Saved Audience through interest targeting, demographics, and geography.

My music academy has a number of students in the California Home School system. I use the Saved Audience to choose parents with home-schooled children ages 6 to 18 who are interested in home schools and music education. I then target down to a 12-mile radius around my school. I then "save" this audience to run future ads to them.

I can also create audiences with slightly different interests, such as musical theatre or readers of *Backstage Magazine*. Testing different combinations helps me pinpoint my most profitable audiences.

I then run ads enticing them with interesting content in order to get them to click over to my website, where they are pixeled. These visitors then go into my Custom Audience to be sent retargeting ads asking for a sale or pushing them further into my sales funnel.

Using the Saved Audiences and pinpointing their interests gives me a constant supply of new people to show my ads to at a better cost than any other advertising I have ever tried. Plus, the better job you do of keeping people interested in your ads, the less Facebook charges you to show them.

This is why the avatar is so important: it allows us to really focus on running ads to the right people where the likelihood of them being interested is high.

Avoiding Account Shutdown

The worst thing that can happen to your Facebook account is the dreaded shutdown. Since Facebook owns the playing field, they can kick you out at any time.

Facebook wants the user experience to be a positive one (so they keep coming back) and has certain rules to make sure advertisers keep the experience positive as well.

You cannot make wild promises, such as doubling your vocal range overnight. You can't call out specific medical issues, such as people with nodules or acid reflux. Part of the reason for this is Facebook doesn't want users to know the amount of private information they hold. These rules are mainly for medical and health services advertisers, but you should be aware of them.

You also cannot do a bait-and-switch where you promise free information in your ad yet the link simply goes to a sales page—you must link to and deliver what is promised in the ad.

The page you link to should also have your contact information (because Facebook wants to make sure you are a legit business) as well as NO annoying popups that stop people from leaving.

It is advisable to stay up-to-date with Facebook's latest policies. As the page can change, I recommend Googling "Facebook advertiser policies."

Facebook will also offer you the opportunity to run your ads on a connected Instagram account, which I highly recommend. Between Facebook and Instagram, you are covering most social media usage.

Using Social Media

To paraphrase a popular biblical teaching: be in social media, but not of it.

Facebook employs behavioral scientists who are experts in doing one thing: grabbing your attention and keeping it. Social media is engineered to be an addicting time-waster, and your attention is what Facebook sells to advertisers.

If you are going to build your influence, you need to become adept at utilizing social media to build your business—but you also need to avoid its traps, or you will find your time and productivity adversely affected.

I have a major rule for myself: I NEVER, EVER argue with someone online. It will suck you in and consume your emotional energy. There is little to be gained by debating the usage of a popular singing term (or even worse, politics), especially if you are not interested in learning something new but merely defending your current position.

Who cares if someone in Akron, Ohio thinks you are a hack for using the term "chest voice?" (This exact thing happened to me). What do you gain by convincing them otherwise? Remember, the value of your time is at least $200 an hour, and engaging in these arguments is absolutely worthless.

I recently found myself spending more and more time on Twitter, watching the bloodbath of arguments that is the Twittershpere. I realized this was not an effective use of my time, so I removed Twitter from my phone.

I have also removed Facebook from my phone. What, you say? I found it too easy to pick up my phone at random moments and go down that non-productive hole. Remember, these apps are designed by very smart people to addict us. I now only use Facebook on my laptop, and only for specific business purposes such as posting or research. I even purchased special software so I can do Facebook Live broadcasts from my laptop.

Speaking of your phone, learn to put it away (i.e., in another room) when you are working. I also turn off all alerts on my computer during my focused work times.

I am often asked how I seem to create so much content and get a great deal done. Eliminating distraction is a huge part of my strategy. I highly suggest you remove all distractions when working as well.

If you would like more productivity tips, I have created a bonus chapter for you in the member's area for this book johnhenny.com/bookbonus

By utilizing social media strategically, without getting pulled into its time-wasting orbit, you can quickly grow your audience and income.

Chapter Twenty
OUTSOURCING

As you begin to grow your influence and business, something unexpected will happen … you will have *less* free time, not more. Before long, you will begin to feel overwhelmed with trying to keep up with your teaching load as well as your content creation, marketing, product development, etc.

This is where the next big step comes in—outsourcing.

So much of what you need to do can be done by others relatively inexpensively, without the need for employees, payroll taxes, etc. You can find virtual assistants and technical people to do just about any job you would need. The key is to know what you need to do yourself and what should be given to others.

Do The $200-An-Hour Jobs

Your time has value, and it is likely much more than you think. Once you build up your studio and product, your time could be worth hundreds if not thousands of dollars per hour. Let me explain.

I can teach private voice for an hour, and I am able to charge a healthy rate because I am in Los Angeles. I can make a nice living, but there are jobs I can do that bring in much more potential revenue.

If I take a block of time and spend it creating a new education product, I am able to potentially earn far more for those hours than my teaching rate.

But if I spend my non-teaching hours handling all the small jobs of scheduling students or editing my videos, I have now drastically reduced my overall hourly earning rate.

These little jobs can be handled very well for around $10 per hour, which leaves me free to do the jobs that can generate much more.

Which jobs should you spend your precious time doing?

I believe if you take the concepts of this book and apply them (by creating services and products that reach a greater number of singers and performers), your hourly earning potential will skyrocket.

You are worth a minimum of $200 per hour, much likely more. Now, I'm not telling you to charge your private students that much, but I want to make you very aware of how you spend your working hours and what the potential of these hours really is.

I am spending a good deal of hours writing this book, and as I sit typing, I get no immediate financial reward for doing so. But here's what I do know.

These words will reach those who are of like mind and ambition—someone like you. And some of you are going to get a fire in the belly to take your studio and teaching as far as you can, and you will want to invest in getting there more quickly. There will be a number of teachers reading this who will want to work with me on a deeper level. Some will buy a course, and some will invest in one-on-one coaching.

In this bigger picture, every hour I happily sit here writing is earning me potential revenue. In order to carve out this productive and profitable writing time, I need to delegate the sub-$200 per hour jobs elsewhere. I simply lose money every time I engage in them, and so do you.

The key to increased revenue and profit with the allotted work hours you have is outsourcing—hiring virtual assistants and key project people for tasks you shouldn't be handling.

Make a list of all the various tasks you might have to do in a workday.

Mine would look something like this:

- Schedule students
- Return phone calls
- Deal with rescheduling
- Answer questions for potential students
- Email my list
- Social media posts
- Teach lessons
- Record podcast
- Edit and upload podcast
- Create a podcast page
- Product customer service including refunds, changing credit cards, issues logging in, etc.
- Record product videos
- Edit product videos
- Build a product framework
- Create Facebook Ads
- Monitor Facebook Ads
- Write blogs
- Create lead magnet giveaways
- Design landing page
- Website maintenance

Out of all these tasks, there are only a handful I need to do myself. I decide what is critical for me to handle and then allow others to do the small jobs, which increases my efficiency and productivity, as well as my profits and my overall hourly rate.

The tasks I do are the ones I find most important to myself and my clients. They are:

- Teaching my students (but not scheduling, answering emails, getting payment, etc.)
- Writing blog posts (but not formatting, doing SEO, etc.)
- Giving public lectures and masterclasses
- Creating and recording course and education content (but not editing, etc.)
- Reading, researching, and growing my professional knowledge
- Overseeing growth and marketing of my music academy and product line

The one area I still hang on to quite strongly is the marketing. There are a couple of reasons: First, there is no one who will understand my business like I do, and no one will understand my customer the same.

Second, letting someone else run your marketing can get expensive very quickly. At the very least you should learn the nuts and bolts of basic marketing and sales and be fluent in how to run a Facebook Ad campaign. This way you can oversee exactly how your ad dollars are being spent and kill any underperforming ads very quickly.

How To Start Outsourcing

I suggest starting with small, one-off jobs until you get the hang of the workflow and training others.

I particularly like Fiverr for this purpose. While you might not find your superstar here, it is very quick and inexpensive, so even if the person you deal with is a total dud it won't cost you very much.

I have used Fiverr for graphic design and video jobs. I had a few times where the work didn't really serve my purposes, and only one time where it was downright lazy and lousy. I was only out $30 for the bad work and I was able to quickly move on and get what I needed from another vendor.

With Fiverr you are dealing with vendors from all over the world who will do your job for as little as $5.

When you are ready for longer-term projects, such as building a new website or creating a product, you will likely want to hire a single person for a longer term.

You have the option of hiring someone local as an employee (often the most expensive) to using a virtual assistant in another part of the globe (often the least expensive).

This depends on your budget as well as your comfort working with others virtually.

Whichever you choose, there is one factor that can make your project a success or doom it to failure: your ability to communicate!

Most jobs fail because the employer does not communicate or train the employee properly. At first, it will be easier and quicker to do something yourself rather than show another how to do it, but this is the trap that keeps us on the $10-an-hour jobs rather than the $200. Don't fall into this.

Use a program such as Snagit to record quick videos of you completing the task and how you want it done. Communicate exactly what you want and don't be afraid to ask for corrections.

The other big mistake is hiring one person to do multiple jobs for which they are not qualified. Your video editor should not be your personal assistant or bookkeeper.

On some of these sites, the applicant will tell you what you want to hear in order to get the job, so if they offer personal assistant duties and you ask them if they can do graphic design, they will likely tell you "yes." It's often a mistake.

Hire each person to do what they do best, and if they don't work out, move on.

Once you get the hang of interviewing, training, and utilizing others to do these $10 jobs, you will wonder how you got by in the first place. You will not only grow your business much faster, but you will get back your free time—and getting your time back is as valuable, or more so, than the profits you will make.

Chapter Twenty-One

FINAL THOUGHTS

This is my Call to Action! I want you to find that fire and excitement of reaching and helping singers all over the world.

I want you to find your voice, your audience, your special gift to all of us—and get that content out there.

If you don't have a product for sale yet, don't worry about it now. The product will come as you build and engage with your audience. They will find you based on the content you offer and will let you know what further content they want.

They will tell you by their views, clicks, comments, and shares. You will learn so much by putting yourself out there.

The biggest source of failure I have seen is lack of action. You now have more knowledge than when you started reading this book. You should have a list of items you want to put into action—the key is in the ACTION.

The slowing and faltering of momentum is a terrible thing. Momentum can push you forward, or it can shrivel like rotting fruit. It really is up to you.

One of the keys to momentum is to surround yourself with like-minded people. Seek out teachers and entrepreneurs who embrace new technology and paradigms, who want to reach beyond their studios, towns, cities, and countries. Teachers who believe knowledge is valuable and should be available to everyone who wants it—both free and paid.

As you embark on this road, you will likely encounter criticism, both from the public as well as from some of your peers. The criticism can be crippling, if you let it. Being around others who share your goals and visions is critical to keep your focus and momentum.

This is the time to not get scared but to get excited. Excited about the work and the learning ahead. Excited for the mistakes you will make and grow from. Excited to start getting better every day and growing your business consistently.

I also don't want you to be a stranger. I would love to hear from you personally at john@johnhenny.com. If you have made it through this book, then I feel you and I have a certain connection. I really want to know what you think and how I can help you achieve your goals.

My favorite comic (back when us old folks would go get the newspaper off the front step) was Calvin and Hobbes. The last strip was published over 25 years ago, and I would like to leave you with Calvin's final line to his faithful stuffed tiger, Hobbes:

"It's a magical world, Hobbes, ol' buddy… Let's go exploring."

WHAT DID YOU THINK?

I want to thank you for taking the time to read *Voice Teacher Influencer*. It is my sincerest wish that this book will continue to be a helpful resource for you and your teaching career.

May I ask you a quick favor?

If you found this book to be helpful, I would very much appreciate your leaving a positive review on Amazon.

Reviews on Amazon really do make a difference in helping others find this book. I also value any and all feedback.

Thank you so much.

John Henny

Printed in Great Britain
by Amazon

19391342R00089